THE KEY TO
THE PROVERBS

RICHARD L. ATKINS

*To John & Jane
with love and blessings
from
Richard Atkins*

© 2020
Published in the United States by Nurturing Faith, Macon, GA.
Nurturing Faith is a book imprint of Good Faith Media (goodfaithmedia.org).
Library of Congress Cataloging-in-Publication Data is available.

ISBN: 978-1-63528-126-2

CONTENTS

PREFACE

Self-help and success-motivation books are currently experiencing a great deal of popularity. People are seeking expert advice in areas that afford them a sense of fulfillment, but this is nothing new. In times past, our forefathers also had these same needs and aspirations. The only difference was that they went to a single source for guidance: the Bible. In that book they found a voice of authority and the expert counsel required to meet their daily needs.

This might still apply today if the Bible could shed some of its mystique and speak more directly to the present-day affairs of men. The Bible has a timeless quality that sets it apart from much that has come from the human pen and tongue, which gives it a headstart over other literature toward achieving a universal appeal.

It is the author's intent that at least one part of the Bible, the Book of Proverbs, should be made attractive to modern readers and, thereby, returned to its rightful place of influence. Accordingly, the canonical collection of Proverbs is presented in a new format and setting, with the author's own artistic illustrations to lend it life. The Bible translation used is the Revised Standard Version, with the exception that the proper name of the Deity is given in its original form as "Yahweh."

Much pick-and-shovel work has been done so that the gems of Proverbs may be more easily gathered without additional digging by the reader.

King Solomon made himself a palanquin ...
(Song of Sol. 3:9)

INTRODUCTION

The Bible is understood by many to be a divine oracle and supernatural voice of authority on the affairs of mankind and the ordering of the universe. While this premise is
valid (that is, the Bible does contain oracles and pronouncements by the Deity), in
many Bible passages the reader can still perceive the human voice of experience offering
practical advice and enlightened opinions instead of divine decrees.

The Book of Proverbs is a good example of the type of scripture predominated
by what some may argue are essentially mundane ideas and admonitions. Certainly, a
minimal degree of divine inspiration was needed by the persons who made the following observations on life:

> A rich man's wealth is his strong city,
>   and like a high wall protecting him.
> (18:11)

> A man's gift makes room for him
>   and brings him before great men.
> (18:16)

> The poor use entreaties,
>   but the rich answer roughly.
> (18:23)

> It is better to live in a corner of the housetop
>   than in a house shared with a contentious woman.
> (21:9, 25:24)

Along with Proverbs, several books of the Bible were anciently set apart by Jewish
scholars and included in a secondary grouping or lesser library of eleven volumes known
in Hebrew as *Ketuvim,* or simply "writings." (In Greek, this is translated as *Hagiographa,*
or "holy writings.") Both titles conveyed the idea that these books presented the worthy
sayings of holy men or sages, which were not necessarily oracles of God such as are
found in the Pentateuch and the Prophets.

The rabbis came to see their religious literature as naturally falling into four strata representing four levels of inspiration. On the topmost level was the most sublime set of scriptures—the Torah, also known as the Five Books of Moses. Next came the Prophets, both major and minor, then the aforementioned Hagiographa. And finally, on the lowest level, were those picturesque commentaries and exhaustive regulations known as the Talmud.

Today, the commonly accepted literary designation for the Hagiographa is "Wisdom Literature," which connotes distilled knowledge and lore as recorded by the Hebrew sages. It follows that these particular writings were concerned with all subjects in which the ancients strove for special insight. For example, the rabbinic sages studied to become wise in "the fear of the Lord," which was to them "the beginning of wisdom" (Prov. 1:7, 9:10). They also collected tribal lore that supposedly disclosed the secrets of natural phenomena and supernatural mysteries.

Being pragmatic about employing their wisdom to practical ends, the composers of proverbs prescribed useful maxims for economic success, accomplishment of social graces, and proficiency in other areas of human relationships. The introductory statement to the Book of Proverbs spelled out the intent and purpose of the book in candid fashion and precise detail:

> That men may know wisdom and instruction,
>   understand words of insight,
>   receive instruction in wise dealing,
>   righteousness, justice, and equity;
>   that prudence may be given to the simple,
>   knowledge and discretion to the youth—
>   the wise man also may hear and increase in learning,
>   and the man of understanding acquire skill,
>   to understand a proverb and a figure,
>   the words of the wise and their riddles.
> (1:2-6)

Wisdom literature is a unique type of Scripture in that it has few references to God, religion, or Israelite history. Thus, it comes closer to being philosophical than theological or ecclesiastical. As the oldest example of Wisdom literature in the Bible (and hence, the most influential on other books of this genre), the Book of Proverbs is worthy of devotional study as well as scholarly analysis.

Collections of wise sayings comprise a very ancient kind of literary form—as is seen in textual materials dating back to early Egyptian and Mesopotamian history—thus linking Wisdom literature with a certain class of people: the professional scribes, counselors, and scholars of antiquity. For this reason, Wisdom literature developed maxims and advice to the young scribe as to how he might attain success and happiness.

Originally, the words "wise" and "wisdom" were broader in meaning, and among the ancients the fact that a person could read and write was taken as evidence of erudition. The word "wisdom" encompassed the skill of the metal worker, the talent of the musician, the craftsmanship of the potter, the curative power of the healer, the accuracy of the archer, the cunning of the magician, the memory of the bard, and the perception of the prophet. Wisdom was, in short, the mastery of any skill or any area of knowledge. Whoever surpassed his peers in an endeavor was "wiser" than they in that area. The ancient astrologer who worked out the movements of the heavens so as to interpret astral "signs" and postulate a primitive cosmology was deemed to be "wise" in the order of God's creation. And the person with enough cunning to solve riddles was no less "wise" than the one who had the shrewdness to advise a ruler on ordering a kingdom or winning a war. Maintaining proper morals was deemed a "wise" course of action, as was the exercise of canny business sense. Knowledge of folklore and divination was "wisdom" no less than the ability to compose proverbs and poetry. And so, with the Book of Proverbs, its treatments on wisdom were in keeping with the philosophy of the times.

The divine origin of wisdom was another peculiar theory of ancient times, wherein the accumulated knowledge and lore of mankind was attributed to specialized gods of wisdom or to semi-divine culture heroes. Wisdom was said to have descended from above upon select men.

With the Hebrews, however, wisdom was manifested uniquely in the supreme Deity (Yahweh) through whose skill the universe was made, and from whose inventiveness the Law—both natural and moral—was derived. Furthermore, God was said to be able to bestow wisdom upon whomever He chose, as He did in the case of Solomon, the titular author of the Book of Proverbs.

> At Gibeon Yahweh appeared to Solomon in a dream by night; and God said, "Ask what I shall give you." And Solomon said ... "Give thy servant ... an understanding mind to govern thy people, that I may discern between good and evil." ... And God said to him ... "Behold, I give you a wise and discerning mind, so that none like you has been before you and none like you shall arise after you."
> (1 Kgs. 3:5, 6a, 9a, 11a, 12b)

One post-captivity writer who contributed a portion of Proverbs, caught up in his litany of devotion to divine Wisdom, threw caution to the winds and introduced the personification of Wisdom as another deity in the Hebrew pantheon. This female figure was extolled as a co-creator with God, the bride of every scholar, and the muse of every artisan (1:20-33, 3:19-20, 8:1-31, 9:1-6).

By contrast, the opponent and evil counterpart of Wisdom was Folly, the seducer of fools and the "strange woman," whose lips dripped honey. Ben Sirach, writing about 180 BC, was obviously influenced by Proverbs when he postulated Wisdom as a female figure whom he equated with the Law:

Wisdom will praise herself
    and will glory in the midst of her people.
In the assembly of the Most High she will open her mouth,
    and in the presence of his host she will glory:
"I came forth from the mouth of the Most High,
    and covered the earth like a mist.
I dwelt in high places,
    and my throne was in a pillar of cloud.
Alone I have made the circuit of the vault of heaven
    and have walked in the depths of the abyss.
In the waves of the sea, in the whole earth,
    and in every people and nation I have gotten a possession.
Among all these I sought a resting place;
    I sought in whose territory I might lodge.
"Then the Creator of all things gave me a commandment,
    and the one who created me assigned a place for my tent.
And he said, 'Make your dwelling in Jacob,
    and in Israel receive your inheritance.'
From eternity, in the beginning, he created me,
    and for eternity I shall not cease to exist.
(Sirach 24:1-9)

The apocryphal Wisdom of Solomon, written about the same time as the book of Sirach, elaborated still further on this theme:

For wisdom is more mobile than any motion;
because of her pureness she pervades and penetrates all things.
For she is a breath of the power of God,   *Simon Magus, a Power*
    and a pure emanation of the glory of the Almighty;   *in Acts 8:9-10*
therefore, nothing defiled gains entrance into her.   *virginal purity*
For she is a reflection of eternal light,
    a spotless mirror of the working of God,
    and an image of his goodness.
Though she is but one, she can do all things,

and while remaining in herself, she renews all things;
in every generation she passes into holy souls
    and makes them friends of God, and prophets;
for God loves nothing so much as the man who lives with wisdom.
For she is more beautiful than the sun   *ref. Rev. 12:1,*
    and excels every constellation of the stars.   *cosmic Sophia*
Compared with the light she is found to be superior,
for it is succeeded by the night,
    but against wisdom evil does not prevail.

She reaches mightily from one end of the earth to the other,
    and she orders all things well.
I loved her and sought her from my youth,
    and I desired to take her for my bride,
    and I became enamored of her beauty.
She glorifies her noble birth by living with God,
    and the Lord of all loves her.
For she is an initiate in the knowledge of God,
    and an associate in his works.
If riches are a desirable possession of life,
    what is richer than wisdom who effects all things?
And if understanding is effective,
    who more than she is fashioner of what exists?
And if any one loves righteousness, her labors are virtues;
    for she teaches self-control and prudence,
    justice, and courage;
    nothing in life is more profitable for men than these.
And if any one longs for wide experience,
    she knows the things of old, and infers the things to come;   *arcane lore*
    she understands turns of speech and the solution of riddles;   *erudition*
    she has foreknowledge of signs and wonders   *omens, portents*
    and of the outcome of seasons and times.   *natural phenomena*
(Wisdom of Solomon 7:24–8:8)

Wisdom was known among the Hellenic Jews by her Greek name, Sophia. As the cosmic mother, Sophia came to be venerated as a full-fledged goddess by later generations of occult gnostics, both Jewish and Christian. (See "Sophia" in the Appendix) Thus, Wisdom was perverted by polytheistic worship into Folly because of an initial, radical preoccupation with all things "wise" in the Book of Proverbs.

In a similar vein, in ancient times "wisdom" was also understood to include folklore, legends, and fables that were passed down by the forefathers. In the pre-scientific era, when inquiries were launched into the unknown, it was easy for the wise man to become transformed into a wizard. Although there is little of this bizarre element in Proverbs, still there is enough of an esoteric aura about the subject of wisdom to cause the name of Solomon to become synonymous with wizardry.

It was a common belief that when Solomon prudently requested wisdom from God in preference to riches and fame, the young ruler obtained a profound depth of wisdom. In fact, he was said to have become almost omniscient, to the point of mastering powerful magic lore. Such was Solomon's occultic fame that he attained the status of a wizard and was numbered among other notable individuals in the legendary literature of the Jews.

The wisest and holiest men were said to be Enoch, Noah, Job, Daniel (actually the Canaanite sage Danel), Ahikar, and the greatest of all seers, Solomon. A quantity of esoteric writings was ascribed to these worthies—much of what survives today under the heading of "pseudepigrapha." Several great men of this caliber were listed in the following Scripture passages.

And God gave Solomon wisdom and understanding beyond measure, and largeness of mind like the sand on the seashore, so that Solomon's wisdom surpassed the wisdom of all the people of the east, and all the wisdom of Egypt. For he was wiser than all other men, wiser than Ethan the Ez'rahite, and Heman, Calcol, and Darda, the sons of Mahol; and his fame was in all the nations round about. He also uttered three thousand proverbs; and his songs were a thousand and five.
(1 Kgs. 4:29-32)

And the word of Yahweh came to me: "Son of man, when a land sins against me by acting faithlessly, and I stretch out my hand against it, and break its staff of bread and send famine upon it, and cut off from it man and beast, even if these three men, Noah, Daniel, and Job, were in it, they would deliver but their own lives by their righteousness."
(Ezek. 14:12-14)

Solomon's reputation as a powerful sorcerer contributed to the fanciful tales that were told about King "Suleiman" in the Qu'ran and in the legends of Arabia. Here, the wizard king was the possessor of a magic staff, a magic ring, and a magic flying carpet. He commanded hordes of demons (or genies) to do his bidding under the spell of great conjurations. It was even reputed that Suleiman's dark minions constructed the

Jerusalem temple overnight without using any tools. Further, they instructed their master in the occult sciences and the arts of divination, much of which came to be recorded in occult manuals or imprinted on magical talismans. By medieval times, "wisdom" had greatly digressed from what we understand it to mean today. Yet although mysticism, magic, gnosticism, cabalism, and occult arts were later to figure prominently in mystical Jewish systems of belief, this was really beyond the scope of the "wisdom" portrayed in the canonical Book of Proverbs.

In theory, Proverbs is an all-inclusive encyclopedia of Near Eastern knowledge; yet, practically it should be noted that some peculiar features of Proverbs may be perceived more by what was omitted than what was included. For example, there are no proverbs dealing with idolatry or sabbath observance—a plain indication that these were settled issues, no longer being violated often enough to warrant treatment. This situation did not occur in Israel until after the end of the Babylonian captivity; hence, the preferred dating of Proverbs to that era—long after the time of Solomon.

Another factor that precludes Solomonic authorship is the way in which the Book of Proverbs personifies Wisdom. The complex development of angelology and the embodiment of an attribute such as Wisdom shows a Persian influence that came long after Solomon's time. In the Persian Zoroastrian faith, concepts such as Truth (*Ashem*), Power (*Kshathrem*), Reverence (*Armaiti*), Perfection (*Haurvatat*), and Immortality (*Ameretat*) were conceived as heavenly beings similar to archangels.

Additionally, the exaltation of righteousness (Prov. 11:3-8, 21:21) does not match with the cynical attitude of one of Solomon's reputed works, the Book of Ecclesiastes. That book advises: "Be not righteous overmuch, and do not make yourself overwise; why should you destroy yourself?" (7:16). Whoever wrote that devious injunction did *not* write the Proverbs.

The composition of the Book of Proverbs has been attributed to Solomon on the authority of the Bible's statement that he "uttered three thousand proverbs; and his songs were a thousand and five" (1 Kgs. 4:32). It is entirely feasible that this wise king did, in fact, form a collection of his most profound sayings, and many of them may well appear in this most eminent example of Hebrew sagacity. But just as all of the Psalms were not composed by David, so it is obvious upon inspection that the Proverbs, too, came from several sources.

One section of Proverbs was written by Lemuel (31:1), another by Agur (30:1), and others by certain "men of Hezekiah" (25:1). Also, some unknown person calling himself "the wise man" (22:17, 24:23) borrowed "thirty sayings" (22:20) from the Egyptian text *Instructions of Amenemopet*, which itself has thirty sections. (See "Proverbs from Egypt" in the Appendix). The fact is, however, that the writers of the Book of Proverbs were for the most part rabbinic sages and elders of the post-captivity Jews. Their style of presentation was that of experienced scholars and practical commentators on life. In works such as Ecclesiastes they could be cynical and skeptical. In later Wisdom literature, such as the Book of Job, the Book of Wisdom (also called "Wisdom of Solomon"), Ecclesiasticus (or "Wisdom of Sirach"), or the Talmud, there occurred an amalgamation with Greek thought from which there emerged a profound philosophy.

But the Book of Proverbs was strictly Jewish. Not significantly influenced by Greek logic, it had no orderly arrangement. Its homespun maxims and humorous, pithy anecdotes were deliberately presented in a helter-skelter fashion. In the Near Eastern way of thinking, a wise man was a bubbling spring of wisdom. Profound precepts, maxims, and parables tumbled from his lips in profusion and at random.

> The words of a man's mouth are deep waters;
> The fountain of wisdom is a gushing stream.
> (Prov. 18:4)

To have arranged the sayings into some logical sequence or into a coherent argument would have nullified the effect of the sages' abundance of knowledge on all subjects. The student who sat at the feet of the Proverbialist was supposed to come away awed by the "shotgun" pattern of great principles aimed at Life, as opposed to the Greek philosopher's "rifle shot" at the target of Truth.

Modern minds have become trained to the Greek viewpoint, however, and the Book of Proverbs no longer grips or convinces us as does a Dialogue of Plato. The lack of systematic arrangement is perceived as a weakness that needs remedy in order to appreciate what the Proverbs are trying to say.

Thus it follows that a grouping of the Proverbs under various headings is the ideal way to achieve a rational coherence of thought. Such a topical treatment provides a very effective key to the Proverbs, opening the way to a modern understanding and appreciation of the book.

The topics considered herein are those subjects that the Jewish sages would have deemed worth discussing, such as advice on ethical issues, business practices, accepted social behavior, charity, and piety. Certainly the Law of Moses as spelled out in the Decalogue would have received primary consideration.

Incline your ear, and hear the words of the wise,
and apply your mind to my knowledge.
(Prov. 22:17a)

AUTHORSHIP OF THE BOOK OF PROVERBS

1:1   The Proverbs of Solomon, son of David, king of Israel.

10:1a   The Proverbs of Solomon.

22:17a   The Words of the Wise: Incline your ear,
and hear and apply your mind to my knowledge.   *ref. pp. 85, 107*

24:23a   These also are sayings of the Wise.

25:1   These also are proverbs of Solomon, which the men
of Hezekiah, king of Judah, copied.

30:1   The Words of Agur, son of Jakeh of Massa.
The man says to Ithiel, to Ithiel and Ucal.   *ref. p. 87*

31:1   The Words of Lemuel, king of Massa,
which his mother taught him.   *ref. pp. 7, 90*

**These also are proverbs of Solomon which
the men of Hezekiah, king of Judah, copied.
(Prov. 25:1)**

THE DECALOGUE

I. Atheism

1:7   The fear of Yahweh is the beginning of knowledge;   *fear: pachad, Gen. 31:42*
         fools despise wisdom and instruction.   *fool: ref. Ps. 14:1*

14:26   In the fear of Yahweh one has strong confidence,
         and his children have a refuge.

14:27   The fear of Yahweh is a Fountain of Life,   *ref. 13:14 (p. 81, 96)*
         that one may avoid the snares of death.   *16:22 (p. 82)*
                                           water of life (nectar),
                           fruit of life (ambrosia) 10:11 (p. 60)

(See "Hebrew Concepts" in the Appendix, p. 96.)

15:33   The fear of Yahweh is instruction in wisdom,
         and humility goes before honor.

30:4   Who has ascended to Heaven and come down?   *divine names:*
         Who has gathered the wind in His fists?   *Hindu* Om
         Who has wrapped up the waters in a garment?   *Hebrew* Yahweh
         Who has established all the ends of the earth?   *"At the Name of Jesus*
         What is His Name, and what is His Son's Name?   *every knee shall bow"*
         Surely you know!   *"Baruch ha Shem Adonai."*
                                  (Bless the Name of the Lord.)

(See "Holy Names of God" in the Appendix, p. 101.)

30:7-9   Two things I ask of thee; deny them not to me before I die:
         Remove far from me falsehood and lying;
         Give me neither poverty nor riches;   *cf. Buddhist desirelessness*
         Feed me with the food that is needful for me,   *"daily bread"*
         Lest I be full, and deny Thee, and say, "Who is Yahweh?"   *the rich*
         Lest I be poor, and steal, and profane the Name of my God.   *hard to enter*
                                                          heaven

II. Idolatry

There are no Proverbs on this subject.   *ref. aniconism of Jews, Muslims*
                                                 This dates Proverbs: written after captivity, so after Solomon.
                                                 Also, there was no need for Jesus to oppose idolatry.

Mica 4-5   Joshua 23,7   Proverb
Deuteronomy 10:20   6-13   37.9

III. Blasphemy

20:25   It is a snare for a man to say rashly, "It is holy,"   *ref. Mark 7:11*
         And to reflect only after making his vows.   *corban, herem vows*

30:9b   ... and profane the Name of my God.   *see 30:9 above under "I. Atheism"*

IV. Sabbath

There are no Proverbs on this subject.   *post-captivity Jews were compliant.*
                                                 This dates Proverbs after the time of Solomon.

V. Family Obligation

1:8-9   Hear, my son, your father's instruction,   *typical poetic parallels*
         And reject not your mother's teaching;
         For they are a fair garland for your head.,   *garland: Gk. stephanos*
         And pendants for your neck.   *ref. p. 77*

(See "Poetic Parallelism in the Hebrew Scriptures" in the Appendix, p. 100.)

4:1   Hear, o sons, a father's instruction,
         And be attentive, that you may gain insight.

10:1b   A wise son makes a glad father,
         But a foolish son is a sorrow to his mother.

11:29   He who troubles his household will inherit the wind,   *"Reap what you sow."*
         And the fool will be servant to the wise.   *"Gone with the wind."*

13:1   A wise son hears his father's instruction,
         But a scoffer does not listen to rebuke.

13:24   He who spares the rod hates his son,
        But he who loves him is diligent to discipline him.

15:20   A wise son makes a glad father,
        But a foolish man despises his mother.

17:2   A slave who deals wisely will rule over a son who acts shamefully,
           and will share the inheritance as one of the brothers.

17:21   A stupid son is a grief to a father;
        And the father of a fool has no joy.

17:25   A foolish son is a grief to his father
        And bitterness to her who bore him.

19:13   A foolish son is ruin to his father,
        And a wife's quarreling is a continual dripping of rain.   *ref. p. 89*

19:18   Discipline your son while there is hope;
        Do not set your heart on his destruction.

19:26-27   He who does violence to his father and chases away his mother
           Is a son who causes shame and brings reproach.
           Cease, my son, to hear instruction
           Only to stray from the words of knowledge.

20:20   If one curses his father or his mother,   *ref. 1 Tim. 5:1*
        His lamp will be put out in utter darkness.   *ref. Rev. 2:5*   19.18

20:29   The glory of young men is their strength,   *respect for elders* 19:25
        But the beauty of old men is their gray hair.
                                                                          10.16

22:6   Train up a child in the way he should go,   *"As the twig is bent ..."*
        And when he is old he will not depart from it.
                                                        Proverbs 27.20

22:15   Folly is bound up in the heart of a child,   "   "   15.11
        But the rod of discipline drives it far from him.
                                                            "   "   21.16
                                                            "   "   13.09
                                                            "   "   24.20
                                                                         15.24

The Name of God, "Yahweh," *is* **God.**

23:13-14   Do not withhold discipline from a child;
           If you beat him with a rod, he will not die.   *Hebrew existentialism:*
           If you beat him with the rod   *save his life, prolong life*
           You will <u>save his life</u> from Sheol.   Sheol *means "death," not "hell."*

23:22   Hearken to your father who begot you,   ⌉   *ref. 2 Tim. 1:13*
           And do not despise your mother when she is old. ⌋

23:26   My son, give me your heart,   Actions speak louder
           And let your eyes observe my ways.   than words.
                                                                 ref. Titus 2:6-8

27:11   Be wise, my son, and make my heart glad,   *ref. 17:6 (p. 38)*
           That I may answer him who reproaches me.   *Preserve the family's honor.*

28:24   He who robs his father or his mother   ⌉
              and says, "That is no transgression,"   ⎬
           Is the companion of a man who destroys.   ⌋

29:15   The rod and reproof give wisdom,
           But a child left to himself brings shame to his mother.

29:17   Discipline your son, and he will give you rest;
           He will give delight to your heart.

29:21   He who pampers his servant from childhood,   *"servant" is slave*
           Will in the end find him his heir.   *Abraham's heir, a slave*
                                                                        Gen. 15:2

30:11   There are those who curse their fathers
           And do not bless their mothers.

30:17   The eye that mocks a father   *ref. Exod. 21:15*
              and scorns to obey a mother
           Will be picked out by the ravens of the valley
              and eaten by the vultures.

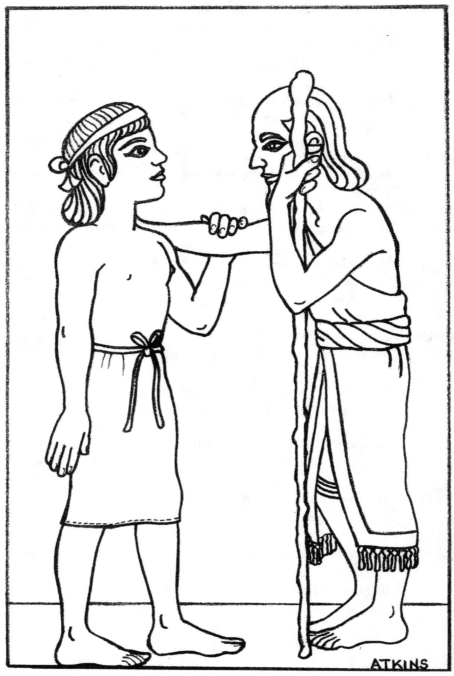

Hearken to your Father who begot you.
(Prov. 23:22)

31:10-31

This is an acrostic poem using the 22 Hebrew letters of the alphabet. Every verse begins
with a successive letter.

א(1)   A good wife who can find?   *Lemuel's checklist for an ideal woman.*
           She is far more precious than jewels.   *Lemuel was cynical about women.*

ב(2)   The heart of her husband trusts in her,   *ref. 31:1-3 (p. 90)*
           And he will have no lack of gain.

ג(3)   She does him good and not harm all the days of her life.

ד(4)   She seeks wool and flax and works with willing hands.

ה(5)   She is like the ships of the merchant;
           She brings her food from afar.   *other acrostics:*

ו(6)   She rises while it is yet night   *Psalm 119 (ref. KJV)*
           And provides food for her household   *Psalm 9–10*
              and tasks for her servant-girls.   *Psalm 25*

ז(7)   She considers a field and buys it;   *Psalm 37*
           With the fruit of her hands she plants a vineyard.   *Lamentations 1–4*

צ(8)   She girds her arms with strength   *Nah. 1:2-10*
             and makes her arms strong.   *ref. mnemonics*

ח(9)   She perceives that her merchandise is profitable.   *and acronyms*
           Her lamp does not go out at night.

י(10)   She puts her hands to the distaff
             and her hands hold the spindle.

כ(11)   She opens her hand to the poor,
             and reaches out her hands to the needy.

ל(12)   She is not afraid of snow for her household,
             for all her household are clothed in scarlet.

מ(13)   She makes herself coverings;
           Her clothing is fine linen and purple.

נ(14)   Her husband is known in the gates
             when he sits among the elders of the land.

ס(15)   She makes linen garments and sells them;
           She delivers girdles to the merchant.

ע(16)   Strength and dignity are her clothing,
           And she laughs at the time to come.

פ(17)   She opens her mouth with wisdom,
           And the teaching of kindness is on her tongue.

ש(18)   She looks well to the ways of her household,
             and does not eat the bread of idleness.

ק(19)   Her children rise up and call her blessed;
            Her husband also, and he praises her:
ר(20)   "Many women have done excellently,
            But you surpass them all."
ש(21)   Charm is deceitful, and beauty is vain,
            But a woman who fears Yahweh is to be praised.
ת(22)   Give her of the fruit of her hands,
            And let her works praise her in the gates.

(See "Alphabetic Acrostics in the Bible" in the Appendix, p. 92.)

She seeks wool and flax
And works with willing hands.
(Prov. 31:13)

VI. Murder and Strife

1:10-19   My son, if sinners entice you, do not consent.
        If they say, "Come with us, let us lie in wait for blood,   *bandit ambush*
         let us wantonly ambush the innocent;
         like Sheol let us swallow them alive and whole,   *earthquakes in Israel*
         like those who go down to the Pit;   *swallowed homes, people*
        we shall find all precious goods, we shall fill our houses with spoil;
        throw in your lot among us; we will all have one purse" —
        My son, do not walk in the way with them,
        Hold back your foot from their paths,
         for their feet run to evil, and they make haste to shed blood.
        For in vain is a net spread in the sight of any bird;
        But these men lie in wait for their own blood;
        They set an ambush for their own lives.
        Such are the ways of all who get gain by violence;   *Criminals kill criminals.*
        It takes away the life of its possessors.   *Police kill criminals.*

3:29-32   Do not plan evil against your neighbor   *To take the sword is*
        who dwells trustingly beside you.   *to perish by the sword.*
        Do not contend with a man for no reason,
        when he has done you no harm.
        Do not envy a man of violence
        and do not choose any of his ways;
        For the perverse man is an abomination to Yahweh,
        But the upright are in His confidence.

6:17   ... haughty eyes, a lying tongue,   *ref. 6:16-19 (p. 60)*
        and hands that shed innocent blood, ...

10:12   Hatred stirs up strife, but love covers all offenses.   *cover: kaphar (kippur)*
                                 blood atonement

12:16   The vexation of a fool is known at once,
        But the prudent man ignores an insult.

14:17   A man of quick temper acts foolishly,
        But a man of discretion is patient.

14:29   He who is slow to <u>anger</u> has great understanding,
         But he who has a hasty temper exalts folly.

15:1   A soft answer turns away wrath,
         But a harsh word stirs up <u>anger</u>.

15:18   A hot-tempered man stirs up strife,   *ref. Matt. 5:21-22*
         But he who is slow to <u>anger</u> quiets contention.

16:32   He who is slow to <u>anger</u> is better than the mighty,
         And he who rules his spirit than he who takes a city.   *conquer self*

17:9   He who forgives an offense seeks love,
         But he who repeats a matter alienates a friend.

17:14   The beginning of strife is like letting out water,
         So quit before the quarrel breaks out.

17:19   He who loves transgression loves strife;
         He who makes his door high seeks destruction.   *unstable door*
                                                                          collapses

19:11   Good sense makes a man slow to <u>anger</u>,
         And it is his glory to overlook an offense.

20:3   It is an honor for a man to keep aloof from strife,   *"fool": Heb.* kesil
         But every <u>fool</u> will be quarreling.

22:10   Drive out a scoffer, and strife will go out,
         And quarreling and abuse will cease.

22:24-25 Make no friendship with a man given to <u>anger</u>,
         nor go with a wrathful man,
         Lest you learn his ways
             and entangle yourself in a snare.

24:8   He who plans to do evil will be called a mischief-maker.

25:23   The north wind brings forth rain;   *wind brings rain*
         And a backbiting tongue, <u>angry</u> looks.   *fire brings smoke*

25:28   A man without self-control
          is like a city broken into and left without walls.

26:17   He who meddles in a quarrel not his own
          is like one who takes a passing dog by the ears.   *"Let sleeping dogs lie."*

27:3-6   A stone is heavy and sand is weighty,
          But a fool's provocation is heavier than both.
          Wrath is cruel, anger is overwhelming,
          But who can stand before jealousy?
          Better is open rebuke
          Than hidden love.
          Faithful are the wounds of a friend;
          Profuse are the kisses of an enemy.   *Judas kiss, hypocrisy*

28:17   If a man is burdened with the blood of another,
          Let him be a fugitive until death;   *pursued by the Furies*
          Let no one help him.

29:22   A man of wrath stirs up strife,
          And a man given to anger causes much transgression.

30:33   For pressing milk produces curds,
          Pressing the nose produces blood,
          And pressing anger produces strife.

VII. Adultery

2:16-19   You will be saved from the loose woman,   *cf. Eve's seduction of Adam*
          From the adventuress with her smooth words,   *adventure: seek new, different.*
          Who forsakes the companion of her youth   *ref. child marriage*
          And forgets the covenant of her God;   *marriage vows*
          For her house sinks down to death and her paths to the shades;
          None who go to her come back,
          Nor do they regain the paths of life.

5:3-20   For the lips of a loose woman drip honey,
          And her speech is smoother than oil;
          But in the end she is bitter as wormwood,

Profuse are the kisses of an enemy.
(Prov. 27:6)

Sharp as a two-edged sword.
Her feet go down to death;
Her steps follow the path to Sheol.
She does not take heed to the path of life;
Her ways wander, and she does not know it.

And now, O sons, listen to me,
And do not depart from the words of my mouth:
Keep your <u>way</u> far from her,   *"way": thigh or loins*
   and do not go near the <u>door</u> of her house;   *Gen. 24:2, 47:29*
Lest you give your honor to others,   *open "door" (Song of Sol. 8:9)*
   and your years to the merciless;   *"door": female anatomy*
Lest strangers take their fill of your <u>strength</u>,   *"strength" to oldest son*
   and your <u>labors</u> go to the house of an outcast;   *Gen. 49:3. Labors: vigor*
And at the end of your life you groan,   *ref. 31:3 (p. 90)*
   when your flesh and body are consumed.   *Old superstition:*
And you say,   *sex depletes power*
"How I hated discipline,   *and ages the body.*
And my heart despised reproof!   *Sexual lassitude foretells death:*
I did not listen to the voice of my teachers   *some animals spawn and die.*
   or incline my ear to my instructors.
I was at the point of utter ruin
In the assembled congregation."

Drink water from your own <u>cistern</u>,   *"cistern," "well":*
   flowing water from your own <u>well</u>.   *female sexual anatomy*
Should your <u>springs</u> be scattered abroad,   *onanism (Gen. 38:9)*
   streams of water in the streets?
Let them be for yourself alone
And not for strangers with you.
Let your <u>fountain</u> be blessed,   *"fountain": male sexual anatomy*
And rejoice in the wife of your youth,
   a lovely hind, a graceful doe.
Let her breasts satisfy you at all times with delight;
Be infatuated always with her love.
Why should you be infatuated, my son, with a loose woman
And embrace the bosom of an adventuress?

ISAIH 51.1
ISIAH

6:24-35   ...to preserve you from the evil woman,
           From the smooth tongue of the adventuress.
           Do not desire her beauty in your heart,
           And do not let her capture you with her eyelashes;
           For a harlot may be hired for a loaf of bread,   *Better a harlot than*
           But an adulteress stalks a man's very life.   *another man's wife.*
           Can a man carry fire in his bosom and his clothes not be burned?
           Or can one walk upon hot coals and his feet not be scorched?
           So is he who goes in to his neighbor's wife;
           None who touches her will go unpunished.
           Do not men despise a thief if he steals   *stealing a man's wife:*
              to satisfy his appetite when he is hungry?   *his property, "chattel"*
           And if he is caught, he will pay seven-fold;   *ref. 6:30 (p. 17)*
           He will give all the goods of his house.
           He who commits adultery has no sense;   *"without a heart": chaser leb*
           He who does it destroys himself.   *ref. 15:21 (p. 82)*
           Wounds and dishonor will he get,
           And his disgrace will not be wiped away.
           For jealousy makes a man furious,
           And he will not spare when he takes revenge.
           He will accept no compensation,
           Nor be appeased though you multiply gifts.

7:5-27   ... to preserve you from the loose woman,
           From the adventuress with her smooth words.
           For at the window of my house
           I have looked out through my lattice,
           And I have seen among the simple,
           I have perceived among the youths,
              a young man without sense,   *Footprints in the sidewalk at*
              passing along the street near her corner,   *Ephesus show the way to*
              taking the road to her house   *a house of prostitutes.*
              in the twilight, in the evening,
              at the time of night and darkness.
           And lo, a woman greets him, dressed as a harlot, wily of heart.
           She is loud and wayward; her feet do not stay at home;
           Now in the street, now in the market,
              and at every corner she lies in wait.
           She seizes him and kisses him, and with impudent face

She says to him:
"I had to offer sacrifices,   *cf.* mikveh *bath after*
And today I have paid my vows: *monthly impurity*
So now I have come out to meet you,
To seek you eagerly, and I have found you.
I have decked my couch with coverings,
    colored spreads of Egyptian linen;
I have perfumed my bed with myrrh, aloes, and cinnamon.
Come, let us take our fill of love till morning;
Let us delight ourselves with love.
For my husband is not at home;
He has gone on a long journey;
He took a bag of money with him;
At full moon he will come home."
With much seductive speech she persuades him;
With her smooth talk she compels him.
All at once he follows her, as an ox goes to the slaughter,
    or as a stag is caught fast till an arrow pierces its entrails;
    or as a bird rushes into a snare;
He does not know that it will cost him his life.
And now, O sons, listen to me,
And be attentive to the words of my mouth.
Let not your heart turn aside to her ways;
Do not stray into her paths;
For many a victim has she laid low;
Yea, all her slain are a mighty host.
Her house is the way to Sheol,   Sheol *divided into cells (cf. many mansions)*
    going down to the <u>chambers of death</u>.   *ref. 21:16 (p. 39)*

9:13-18   A foolish woman is noisy;   *cf.* Wisdom's cry, *1:20 (p. 73)*
          She is wanton and knows no shame.
          She sits at the door of her house;
          She takes a seat on the high places of the town,   *Rahab lived in a house*
              calling to those who pass by,   *on the city wall.*
              who are going straight on their way,
          "Whoever is simple, let him turn in here!"
          And to him who is <u>without sense</u> she says,   *"without a heart":* chaser leb
          "Stolen water is sweet,
              and bread eaten in secret is pleasant."

ATKINS

Come, let us take our fill of love ...
(Prov. 7:18)

       But he does not know that the dead are there,
         that her guests are in the depths of Sheol.

12:4   A good wife is the crown of her husband,
         But she who brings shame is like rottenness in his bones.   *bone cancer*

14:1   Wisdom builds her house,
         But Folly with her own hands tears it down.   *ref. 14:1 (p. 89)*

22:14   The <u>mouth</u> of a loose woman is a deep <u>pit</u>;   *sexual imagery*
         He with whom Yahweh is angry will fall into it.   *determinism:*
                                      "Lead us not to temptation."

23:27-28 For a harlot is a deep <u>pit</u>;   *"pit," "well": female anatomy*
         An adventuress is a narrow <u>well</u>.
         She lies in wait like a robber
         And increases the faithless among men.   *gives a bad reputation*

29:3   He who loves wisdom makes his father glad,
         But one who keeps company with harlots squanders his <u>substance</u>.
                   "substance," "natural force": semen (Deut. 34:7)
                   youthful semen gives strong sons. ref. 5:10 (p. 13)

30:20   This is the way of an adventuress: *double entendre:*
         She eats and wipes her <u>mouth</u>, and says,   *female sexual anatomy*
         "I have done no wrong."

VIII. Thievery

6:30-31 Do not men despise a thief if he steals   *(... a wife)*
           to satisfy his appetite when he is hungry?   *ref. VII. Adultery (p. 11)*
         And if he is caught, he will pay sevenfold;   *cf. Lamech (Gen. 4:23-24)*
         He will give all the goods of his house.

20:10   Diverse weights and diverse measures   *ref. 11:1 (p. 35)*
         Are both alike an abomination to Yahweh.   *ref. 16:11 (p. 37)*

20:23   Diverse weights are an abomination to Yahweh,   *scales now certified*
         And false scales are not good.   *by gov't inspectors*

21:6-7   The getting of treasures by a lying tongue
          Is a fleeting vapor and a snare of death.
          The violence of the wicked will sweep them away,
          Because they refuse to do what is just.

22:22-23 Do not rob the poor, because he is poor,   *ref. 14:31 (p. 46)*
          Or crush the afflicted at the gate;   *afflicted: lepers*
          For Yahweh will plead their cause
          And despoil of life those who despoil them.

25:4   Take away the dross from the silver,   *ref. refiner's fire (Mal. 3:2)*
          And the smith has material for a vessel.   *purgatory (1 Cor. 3:12-15)*

28:8   He who augments his wealth by interest and increase   *usury:*
          Gathers it for him who is kind to the poor.   *Exod. 22:25, Deut. 23:19-20*

29:24   The partner of a thief hates his own life;
          He hears the curse, but discloses nothing.   *curse: sentencing*

IX. Falsehood and Truth

3:3   Let not loyalty and faithfulness forsake you;   *traitors: Ahithophel, Judas*
          Bind them about your neck;   *—in Dante's lowest pit of hell*
          Write them on the tablet of your heart.   *2 Sam. 17:1, Ps. 41:9, Matt. 27:5*

6:12-15   A worthless person, a wicked man,
          Goes about with crooked speech,   *crooked speech: forked tongue*
          Winks with his eyes,
          Scrapes with his feet,   *obsequious, devious, Uriah Heep*
          Points with his finger,
          With perverted heart   *goddess Discord: Eris, sister of Mars,*
             devises evil, continually sowing <u>discord</u>;   *mother of Strife*
          Therefore, calamity will come upon him suddenly;
          In a moment he will be broken beyond healing.   *Judas hanged himself,*
                                                         also Ahithophel (2 Sam. 17:23)

6:19   ... a false witness who breathes out lies,
          And a man who sows <u>discord</u> among brothers.

10:18-21   He who conceals hatred has lying lips,   *an ulterior motive*
            And he who utters <u>slander</u> is a fool.   *malicious defamation of*
            When words are many, transgression is not lacking,   *character, reputation*
            But he who restrains his lips is prudent.
            The tongue of the righteous is choice silver;
            The mind of the wicked is of little worth.
            The lips of the righteous feed many,
            But fools die for lack of sense.

10:32   The lips of the righteous know what is acceptable,   *eloquence in the tongue*
            But the mouth of the wicked, what is perverse.   *knowledge in the lips*
                                                                     See "Hebrew Man," p. 83

11:9   With his mouth the godless man would destroy his neighbor,   *the atheist*
            But by knowledge the righteous are delivered.   *has no reason to be moral*

Diverse weights and diverse measures
Are both alike an abomination to Yahweh.
(Prov. 11:1, 16:11, 20:10)

11:12-13   He who belittles his neighbor lacks sense,
         But a man of understanding remains silent.   *words spoken*
         He who goes about as a talebearer reveals secrets,   *in confidence*
         But he who is trustworthy in spirit keeps a thing hidden. *are given in trust*

12:5-6   The thoughts of the righteous are just;   *Arabic* taqiyya: *lying to an*
         The counsels of the wicked are <u>treacherous</u>. *infidel is acceptable to Allah.*
         The words of the wicked lie in wait for blood, *promises, treaties broken*
         But the mouth of the upright delivers men.

12:12-14   The strong tower of the wicked comes to ruin,   *lookout tower:* migdol
         But the root of the righteous stands firm.   *root: foundation*
         An evil man is ensnared by the transgression of his lips,
         But the righteous escapes from trouble.
         From the fruit of his words a man is satisfied with good, *words of the mouth*
         And the work of a man's hand comes back to him. *works of the hand*
                                                       (good or evil)

12:17-23   He who speaks the truth gives honest evidence,
         But a false witness utters deceit.
         There is one whose rash words are like sword thrusts, *Jas. 3:5-10*
         But the tongue of the wise brings healing.   *Rev. 1:16*
         Truthful lips endure for ever,   *ref. 18:21 (p. 21)*
         But a lying tongue is but for a moment.
         Deceit is in the heart of those who devise evil,
         But those who plan good have joy.
         No ill befalls the righteous,   *divine bias*
         But the wicked are filled with trouble.   *ref. 22:2, 22:7 (p. 54)*
         Lying lips are an abomination to Yahweh,   *28:21 (p. 41)*
         But those who act faithfully are His delight.
         A prudent man conceals his knowledge,
         But <u>fools</u> proclaim their folly.   *"fool": Heb.* kesil *(p. 96)*

13:2-3   From the fruit of his mouth a good man eats good,
         But the desire of the treacherous is for violence.
         He who guards his mouth preserves his life;
         He who opens wide his lips comes to ruin.

13:5   A righteous man hates falsehood,
         But a wicked man acts shamefully and disgracefully.

13:17	A bad messenger plunges men into trouble,	*Uriah carried a message*
	But a faithful envoy brings healing.	*of his own doom (2 Sam. 11:14).*

14:5   A faithful witness does not lie,
But a false witness breathes out lies.

14:15   The <u>simple</u> believes everything,   *"simple": Heb.* pethi *(p. 96)*
But the prudent looks where he is going.   *credulous, gullible, naive*

14:25   A truthful witness saves lives,
But one who utters lies is a betrayer.

15:4   A gentle tongue is a <u>Tree of Life</u>,   *ref. 3:18 (p. 75), 11:30 (p. 61)*
But perverseness in it breaks the spirit.   *13:12 (p. 32)*

16:27-30 A <u>worthless</u> man <u>plots evil,</u>   *Belial: Worthless (a name for the Devil)*
And his speech is like a <u>scorching fire.</u>   *Onesimus: Useful (Phil. 10-11)*
A perverse man <u>spreads strife,</u>
And a <u>whisperer</u> separates close friends.
A <u>man of violence</u> entices his neighbor
And leads him in a way that is not good.
He who winks his eyes plans <u>perverse things;</u>
He who compresses his lips brings evil to pass.

17:4   An evildoer <u>listens to wicked lips;</u>
And a liar gives heed to a <u>mischievous tongue.</u>

17:7   Fine speech is not becoming to a fool;
Still less is false speech to a prince.

17:20   A man of <u>crooked mind</u> does not prosper,
And one with a <u>perverse tongue</u> falls into calamity.

18:8   The words of a whisperer are like delicious morsels;   *ref. 26:22 (p. 24)*
They go down into the inner parts of the body.

18:20-21 From the fruit of his mouth a man is satisfied;
He is satisfied by the yield of his lips.
Death and life are in the power of the tongue,
And those who love it will eat its fruits.

19:1   Better is a poor man who walks in his integrity
        Than a man who is perverse in speech, and is a fool.

19:5   A false witness will not go unpunished,
        And he who utters lies will not escape.

19:9   A false witness will not go unpunished,
        And he who utters lies will perish.

19:22   What is desired in a man is loyalty,   *In heraldry, blue means loyalty.*
        And a poor man is better than a liar.   *It is "true blue."*

19:28   A worthless witness mocks at justice,
        And the mouth of the wicked devours iniquity.

20:17   Bread gained by deceit is sweet to a man,   *Rev. 10:9-10. Grace is sweet.*
        But afterward his mouth will be full of gravel.   *Self-denial is bitter.*

20:19   He who goes about gossiping reveals secrets;   *Matt. 7:6*
        Therefore do not associate with one who speaks foolishly.   *1 Cor. 5:1-2*

21:23   He who keeps his mouth and his tongue
        Keeps himself out of trouble.

21:28   A false witness will perish,
        But the word of a man who hears will endure.

23:23   Buy truth and do not sell it;   *Buy the pearl of great price.*
        Buy wisdom, instruction, and understanding.   *Matt. 13:46*

25:13   Like the cold of snow in the time of harvest
        Is a faithful messenger to those who send him;
        He refreshes the spirit of his masters.

25:18-19 A man who bears false witness against his neighbor
          Is like a war club, or a sword, or a sharp arrow.
          Trust in a faithless man in time of trouble
          Is like a bad tooth or a foot that slips.

The words of a whisperer are like delicious morsels.
(Prov. 18:8, 26:22)

26:18-25   Like a madman who throws firebrands, arrows, and death,
            Is the man who deceives his neighbor and says,
            "I am only joking!"
            For lack of wood the fire goes out,   *ref. 15:1 (p. 10)*
            And where there is no whisperer, quarreling ceases.
            As charcoal to hot embers and wood to fire,
            So is a quarrelsome man for kindling strife.
            The words of a whisperer are like delicious morsels;   *ref. 18:8 (p. 21)*
            They go down into the inner parts of the body.
            Like the glaze covering an earthen vessel
            Are smooth lips with an evil heart.
            He who hates, dissembles with his lips
            and harbors deceit in his heart;
            When he speaks graciously, believe him not,
            For there are seven abominations in his heart.   *Luke 8:2, Mary Magdalene*

26:28   A lying tongue hates its victims,
            And a flattering mouth works ruin.

27:14   He who blesses his neighbor with a loud voice,
                rising early in the morning,
            Will be counted as cursing.

28:23   He who rebukes a man will afterward find more favor
            ... than he who flatters with his tongue.

29:5   A man who flatters his neighbor spreads a net for his feet.

30:7   Remove far from me falsehood and lying.   *ref. 30:7-9 (p. 1)*

X. Covetousness

24:1-2   Be not envious of evil men, nor desire to be with them;   *ref. 23:17 (p. 64)*
            For their minds devise violence, and their lips talk of mischief.

24:19   Fret not yourself because of evildoers,
            And be not envious of the wicked.   *cf. Buddhist desirelessness*

27:20   Sheol and Abaddon are never satisfied,   *ref. 15:11 (p. 37)*
            And never satisfied are the eyes of man.   *Hades and Perdition (ruin)*

30:15-16   The <u>leech</u> has two daughters;   *clinger, blood-sucker*

                "Give, give," they cry.
                Three things are never satisfied;
                Four never say, "Enough":   *Early superstition:*
                Sheol,   *When Sheol, the womb*
                The barren womb,   *of mother Earth is full,*
                The earth ever thirsty for water,   *the world will end.*
                And the fire, which never says, "Enough."

Third Heaven
("Heaven of Heavens")
The House of the High God

Second Heaven
The higher gods, the *Igigi*,
are depicted by their animal
symbols and altar standards.

First Heaven
The lower gods, the *Anunnaki*,
nature powers, are shown with
monster guardians.

A Firmament

The Luminaries
Venus, Moon, Sun, Lightning
(Fire)

The Resevoir of Rain
The "waters above the
firmament"

The Cosmic Serpent
The dragon Tiamat in the
nether Deep supports the
world and the pillars of a
multi-tiered heaven.

THE ANCIENT COSMOS

A Babylonian Boundary Marker depicts the universe as it was conceived by the ancients (British Museum). (See also the ancient boundary marker, page 56.)

FATE

16:1   The plans of the mind belong to man,   *"Man proposes; God disposes"*
            But the answer of the tongue is from Yahweh.   *ref. 19:21 (p. 84)*

                  所 heart

16:9   A man's mind plans his way,
            But Yahweh directs his steps.   *determinism*

16:33   The lot is cast into the lap,   *ref. 18:18 (p. 38)*
            But the decision is wholly from Yahweh.   Urim*: Num. 27:21*

20:24   A man's steps are ordered by Yahweh;   *Determinism is*
            How then can man understand his way?   *inscrutible.*

21:1   The king's heart is a stream of water in the hand of Yahweh;   *determinism*
            He turns it wherever He will.   *God directs and decides fate of nations.*

27:1   Do not boast about tomorrow,   *Matt. 6:34*
            For you do not know what a day may bring forth.

The lot is cast into the lap,
But the decision is wholly from Yahweh.
(Prov. 16:33)

GOVERNMENT

16:10   Inspired decisions are on the lips of a king;
His mouth does not sin in judgment.   *ref. 28:28, 29:2, 29:16 (p. 65)*

16:12-15 It is an abomination to kings to do evil,
For the throne is established by righteousness.
Righteous lips are the delight of a king,
And he loves him who speaks what is right.
A king's wrath is a messenger of death,   *dread autocracy, monarchy*
And a wise man will appease it.
In the light of the king's face there is life,
And his favor is like the clouds that bring the spring rain.

17:7   Fine speech is not becoming to a fool;   *social strata. ref. 19:10 (p. 84)*
Still less is false speech to a prince.

19:12   A king's wrath is like the growling of a lion,   *like the hiss of*
But his favor is like dew upon the grass.   *a snake in the grass*

20:2   The dread wrath of a king is like the growling of a lion;
He who provokes him to anger forfeits has life.

20:8   A king who sits on the throne of judgment
winnows all evil with his eyes.   *cf. the hypnotic gaze of Billy Graham*

20:18   Plans are established by counsel;
By wise guidance wage war.   *warfare normal*

20:26   A wise king winnows the wicked   *millstone grinding,*
and drives the wheel over them.   *threshing wheel and chariot wheel*

20:28   Loyalty and faithfulness preserve the king,
And his throne is upheld by righteousness.

22:11   He who loves purity of heart
And whose speech is gracious
Will have the king as his friend.

24:21-22 My son, fear Yahweh and the king,   *God and Caesar*
And do not disobey either of them,
For disaster from them will rise suddenly,
And who knows the ruin that will come from them both?

25:2-3   It is the glory of God to conceal things,   *mystery necessary to religion?*
But the glory of kings is to search things out.   *cf. the wisdom of Solomon*
As the heavens for height,
And the earth for depth,
So the mind of kings is unsearchable.   *ruler's ethics not to be questioned*

25:5-8   Take away the wicked from the presence of the king,
And his throne will be established in righteousness.
Do not put yourself forward in the king's presence
Or stand in the place of the great,
For it is better to be told, "Come up here,"   *Jas. 2:3*
Than to be put lower in the presence of the prince.
What your eyes have seen do not hastily bring into court,
For what will you do in the end,
When your neighbor puts you to shame?

25:15   With patience a ruler may be persuaded,
And a soft tongue will break a bone.

28:2   When a land transgresses, it has many rulers,   *Israel, a buffer state,*
But with men of understanding and knowledge   *often invaded.*
Its stability will long continue.

28:15-16 Like a roaring lion or a charging bear
Is a wicked ruler over a poor people.
A ruler who lacks understanding is a cruel oppressor,
But he who hates unjust gain will prolong his days.   *days of reign*

GOVERNMENT

29:4   By justice a king gives stability to the land,
           But one who exacts gifts ruins it.   *bribes; ref. 17:23 (p. 44)*

(See illustration, p. 45.)

29:12   If a ruler listens to falsehood,   *bad counsel leads to a foolish war*
           All his officials will be wicked.

29:14   If a king judges the poor with equity,
           His throne will be established forever.

29:26   Many seek the favor of a ruler,
           But from Yahweh a man gets justice.   *no way to bribe God*

30:29-31 Three things are stately in their tread;   *pomp and majesty*
           Four are stately in their stride: *in nature and*
           The lion, which is the mightiest among beasts   *in government*
           and does not turn back before any,
           The strutting cock,
           The he-goat, and
           A king striding before his people.   *regal procession*

HOPE AND HAPPINESS

13:12   Hope deferred makes the heart sick,
But a desire fulfilled is a <u>Tree of Life</u>.   *ref. 15:4 (p. 21)*

13:19   A desire fulfilled is sweet to the soul,
But to turn away from evil is an abomination to fools.

15:13   A glad heart makes a cheerful countenance,   *ref. 14:13 (p. 36)*
But by sorrow of heart the spirit is broken.

15:15   All the days of the afflicted are evil,   *ref. 11:23 (p. 35)*
But a cheerful heart has a continual feast.

15:23   To make an apt answer is a joy to a man,   *ref. 24:26 (p. 44)*
And a word in season, how good it is!   *Proverb esteemed: 25:11 (p. 86)*

15:30   The light of the eyes rejoices the <u>heart</u>   *ref. 16:21 (p. 82)*
And good news refreshes the <u>bones</u>.   *bodily strength*

16:20   He who gives heed to the word will prosper
And happy is he who trusts in Yahweh.

17:1   Better is a dry morsel with quiet
Than a house full of feasting with strife.

17:22   A cheerful <u>heart</u> is a good medicine,
But a downcast spirit dries up the <u>bones</u>.

18:14   A man's spirit will endure sickness,
But a broken spirit who can bear?

25:20   He who sings songs to a heavy heart   *Eccl. 3:4: "A time to weep."*
Is like one who takes off a garment on a cold day   *Matt. 11:17*
    and like vinegar on a wound.   *(wedding and funeral)*

JUSTICE AND JUDGMENT

1:3   Receive instruction in wise dealing,
          righteousness, justice, and equity.

Proverbs deal with relationships:
courtesy, deference, fairness, liberality.

3:11-12   My son, do not despise Yahweh's discipline
              or be weary of His reproof,
              For Yahweh reproves him whom He loves,
              As a father the son in whom he delights.

One explanation of sorrow:
chastisement from God.

5:21-23   For a man's ways are before the eyes of Yahweh,
              And He watches all his paths.
              The iniquities of the wicked ensnare him,
              And he is caught in the toils of his sin.
              He dies for lack of discipline,
              And because of his great folly he is lost.

ref. 15:3 (p. 36),
22:12 (p. 40)

10:6-7   Blessings are on the <u>head</u> of the righteous,
             But the <u>mouth</u> of the wicked conceals violence.
             The <u>memory</u> of the righteous is a blessing,
             But the <u>name</u> of the wicked will rot.

immortality through
a good name (reputation)
(Shem Tov)

10:17   He who heeds instruction is on the path to life,
            But he who rejects reproof goes astray.

10:27-31   The fear of Yahweh prolongs life,
               But the years of the wicked will be <u>short</u>.
               The hope of the righteous ends in gladness,
               But the expectation of the wicked comes to (nought.)
               Yahweh is a stronghold to him whose way is (upright,)
               But <u>destruction</u> to evildoers.
               The righteous will never be <u>removed</u>,
               But the wicked will not dwell in the land.
               The mouth of the righteous brings forth wisdom,
               But the perverse tongue will be <u>cut off</u>.

Exod. 20:12, long life

ref. Rom. 8:28

Saddiq =
Righteous

ref. 2:21 (p. 58)

If one turns away his ear from hearing the Law,
Even his prayer is an abomination.
(Prov. 28:9)
(See also "Law" p. 42.)

11:1   A false balance is an abomination to Yahweh,   *ref. 20:10 (p. 17)*
            But a just weight is His delight.

11:10-11   When it goes well with the righteous, the city rejoices, *ref. 1:26 (p. 73),*
                                                                      24:17 (40)
            And when the wicked perish there are shouts of gladness. *Schadenfreude*
            By the blessing of the upright a city is exalted,   *corporate favor*
            But it is overthrown by the mouth of the wicked.   *Sodom, Gen. 18:26*

11:18-21   A wicked man earns deceptive <u>wages</u>,   *Rom. 6:23*
            But one who sows righteousness gets a sure <u>reward</u>. *Rom. 8:28*
            He who is steadfast in righteousness will live,
            But he who pursues evil will die.
            Men of perverse mind are an abomination to Yahweh,   *ref. 15:26 (p. 63)*
            But those of blameless ways are His delight.
            Be assured, an evil man will not go unpunished,   *existential justice*
            But those who are righteous will be delivered.   *divine bias*

11:23   The desire of the righteous ends only in <u>good</u>;   *Rom. 8:28*
            The expectation of the wicked is wrath.

11:27   He who diligently seeks <u>good</u> seeks favor,   *divine approval*
            But evil comes to him who searches for it.

11:31   If the righteous is requited on earth,   *existential justice*
            How much more the wicked and the sinner!

12:7   The wicked are overthrown and are no more,   *offspring carry family name*
            But the <u>house</u> of the righteous will stand.   *ref. 17:6 (p. 38)*

13:9   The <u>light</u> of the righteous rejoices,   *ref. 24:20 (p. 40)*
            But the <u>lamp</u> of the wicked will be put out.   *Rev. 2:5*

13:21-22   Misfortune pursues sinners,   *cf. the Furies*
            But prosperity rewards the righteous.
            A good man leaves an inheritance to his children's children,
            But the sinner's wealth is laid up for the righteous.

14:11-14   The <u>house</u> of the wicked will be destroyed,   *house destroyed means;*
           But the tent of the upright will flourish.   *children killed or*
           There is a way which seems right to a man,   *childbirth denied*
           But its end is the way to death.
           Even in laughter the heart is sad,   *survival of the fittest:*
           And the end of joy is grief.   *the righteous.*
           A perverse man will be filled with the fruit of his ways,
           And a good man with the fruit of his deeds.

14:30   A tranquil mind gives life to the flesh,
           But passion makes the bones rot.

14:32   The wicked is overthrown through his evil-doing,
           But the righteous finds refuge through his integrity.

15:3   The eyes of Yahweh are in every place,   *ref. 5:21 (p. 33)*
           Keeping watch on the evil and the good.   *omnipresence*

The eyes of Yahweh are in every place ...   **(Prov. 15:3)**
For a man's ways are before the eyes of Yahweh ...   **(Prov. 5:21)**
The eyes of Yahweh keep watch over knowledge ...   **(Prov. 22:12)**

15:5   A fool despises his father's instruction,
            But he who heeds admonition is prudent.

15:8-12   The sacrifice of the wicked is an abomination to Yahweh,   *God hates sinners.*
            But the prayer of the upright is His delight.   *He ignores their prayers.*
            The way of the wicked is an abomination to Yahweh,   *ref. 15:26 (p. 63)*
            But He loves him who pursues righteousness.
            There is severe discipline for him who forsakes the way;
            He who hates reproof will die.
            Sheol and Abaddon lie open before Yahweh;   *ref. 27:20 (p. 24)*
            How much more the hearts of men!   *Hades and Perdition*
            A scoffer does not like to be reproved;   *"scoffer": Heb.* letz *(p. 96)*
            He will not go to the wise.

15:24   The wise man's path leads upward to life,   *long life before the grave, but*
            that he may avoid Sheol beneath.   *also a hint of immortality*

15:29   Yahweh is far from the wicked,   *God hears no sinner's prayer.*
            But He hears the prayer of the righteous.   *N.T. says He hears, "God, be*
                                                                        merciful to me a sinner." ref. 28:9 (p. 43)

15:31-32   He whose ear heeds wholesome admonition
            Will abide among the wise.
            He who ignores instruction despises himself,
            But he who heeds admonition gains understanding.

16:2-4   All the ways of a man are pure in his own eyes,   *ref. 21:2 (p. 64)*
            But Yahweh weighs the spirit.   *cf. Egyptian judgment scales*
            Commit your work to Yahweh,
            And your plans will be established.   *ref. 16:1 (p. 27), 19:21 (p. 84)*
            Yahweh had made everything for its purpose,   *predestination*
            Even the wicked for the day of trouble.

16:7   When a man's ways please Yahweh,
            He makes even his enemies be at peace with him.

16:11   A just balance and scales are Yahweh's;   *ref. 20:10 (p. 17)*
            All the weights in the bag are His work.

16:25   There is a <u>way</u> which seems right to a man,   *ref. 16:2 (p. 37)*
          But its end is the way to death.

17:3   The crucible is for silver, and the furnace is for gold,   *ref. 1 Cor. 3:11-14*
          And Yahweh tries hearts.

17:6   Grandchildren are the crown of the aged,   *ref. 12:7 (p. 35)*
          And the glory of sons is their fathers.   *27:11 (p. 5)*
                    the righteous receive longevity, prosperity, and progeny: 22:4 (p. 54)

17:11   An evil man seeks only rebellion,   *"messenger": Heb.* malakh
          And a cruel <u>messenger</u> will be sent against him.   *also means "angel"*

17:13   If a man returns evil for good,   *N.T., return good for evil*
          Evil will not depart from his house.   *ref. 20:22 (p. 39)*

17:15   He who justifies the wicked and he who condemns the righteous
          Are both alike an abomination to Yahweh.

17:26   To impose a fine on a righteous man is not good;   *flogging accepted;*
          To <u>flog</u> a noble man is wrong.   *corporal punishment*
                                                                     and public humiliation
18:3   When the wicked comes, contempt comes also,   *for minor crimes;*
          And with dishonor comes disgrace.   *jails and dungeons later.*

18:5-7   It is not good to be partial to a wicked man,
          Or to deprive a righteous man of justice.
          A fool's lips bring strife,
          And his mouth invites a <u>flogging</u>.   *flogging accepted*
          A fool's mouth is his ruin,
          And his lips are a snare to himself.

18:17-19 He who states his case first seems right,   *old forms of litigation*
          Until the other comes and examines him.
          <u>The lot</u> puts an end to disputes   *chance decision, lottery*
          And decides between powerful contenders.   *ref. 16:33 (p. 27)* Urim
          A brother helped is like a strong city,   *Gk.* kleros: lot.
          But quarreling is like the bars of a castle.   *clergy chosen by lot (Luke 1:9)*
                                                                     (cf. allotment)

19:19   A man of great wrath will pay the penalty,
For if you deliver him, you will only have to do it again.

19:25   <u>Strike</u> a <u>scoffer</u>, and the <u>simple</u> will learn prudence;   *flogging accepted*
Reprove a man of understanding, and he will gain knowledge.

19:29   Condemnation is ready for <u>scoffers</u>,   *"scoffer": Heb. letz (p. 96)*
And <u>flogging</u> for the backs of fools.   *"simple": Heb. pethi (p. 96)*

20:22   Do not say, "I will repay evil;"
Wait for Yahweh, and He will help you.   *Deut. 32:35, Rom. 12:19*

20:30   <u>Blows</u> that wound cleanse away evil;   *flogging accepted*
<u>Strokes</u> make clean the innermost parts.

21:3   To do righteousness and justice   *Amos 5:22-24, Micah 6:8,*
    is more acceptable to Yahweh than sacrifice.   *Ps. 51:17, Matt. 5:23-24*

21:11-12   When a <u>scoffer</u> is punished, the <u>simple</u> becomes wise;   *ref. 19:25 above*
When a wise man is instructed, he gains knowledge.
The righteous observes the house of the wicked;
The wicked are cast down to ruin.

21:15-16   When justice is done, it is a joy to the righteous,
But dismay to evildoers.
A man who wanders from the way of understanding   *ref. 7:27 (p. 15)*
Will rest in the <u>assembly of the dead</u>.   *Sheol is qahal raphaim*

21:18   The wicked is a ransom for the righteous,   *God will kill a bad man in*
And the faithless for the upright.   *the place of a good man.*

21:31   The horse is made ready for the day of battle,   *warfare normal.*
But the victory belongs to Yahweh.   *Yahweh is a war God.*
    Exod. 15:3

22:3   A prudent man sees danger and hides himself,   *ref. 27:12 (p. 87)*
But the simple go on and suffer for it.

22:5   Thorns and snares are in the way of the perverse;
        He who guards himself will keep far from them.

22:8   He who sows injustice will reap calamity,   *Gal. 6:7*
        And the rod of his fury will fail.

22:12   The eyes of Yahweh keep watch over knowledge,   *ref. 15:3 (p. 36)*
        But He overthrows the words of the faithless.   *God can void a curse.*

24:16-18 For a righteous man falls seven times and rises again,
          But the wicked are overthrown by calamity.
          Do not rejoice when your enemy falls,   *Schadenfreude*
          And let not your heart be glad when he stumbles,   *ref. 1:26 (p. 73)*
          Lest Yahweh see it and be displeased
              and turn away His anger from him.

24:20   For the evil man has no future,
        The lamp of the wicked will be put out.   *ref. 13:9 (p. 35)*

26:2-3 Like a sparrow in its flitting,
        Like a swallow in its flying,
        A curse that is causeless does not alight.   *Num. 24:10 (Balaam)*
        A whip for the horse, a bridle for the ass,   *ref. 24:28 (p. 44)*
        And a rod for the back of fools.   *flogging accepted*

26:26-27 Though his hatred be covered with guile,
          His wickedness will be exposed in the assembly.
          He who digs a pit will fall into it,   *ref. 28:10 below*
          And a stone will come back upon him who starts it rolling.   *cf. Sisiphus*

28:5   Evil men do not understand justice,
        But those who seek Yahweh understand it completely.

28:10   He who misleads the upright into an evil way
            will fall into his own pit,
        But the blameless will have a goodly inheritance.

28:21   To show partiality is not good,   *Human bias is wrong;*
         But for a piece of bread a man will do wrong.   *God's bias is right.*
                                                                  ref. 12:21 (p. 20)

29:1   He who is often reproved, yet stiffens his neck
            will suddenly be broken beyond healing.

29:19   By mere words a servant is not disciplined,   *flogging necessary*
         For though he understands, he will not give heed.

29:25   The fear of man lays a snare,
         But he who trusts in Yahweh is safe.

31:8-9   Open your mouth for the dumb,
            for the rights of all who are left desolate.

LAW

3:1-2   My son, do not forget my <u>teaching</u>,   *KJV "law": Heb.* torah
But let your heart keep my <u>commandments</u>,   *Heb.* mitsvah
For length of days and years of life   *longevity*
and abundant welfare will they give you.   *prosperity*

4:1-4   Hear, O sons, a father's <u>instruction</u>,   *Heb.* musar
And be attentive, that you may gain insight,
For I give you good <u>precepts</u>;   *KJV "doctrine": Heb.* leqach
Do not forsake my <u>teaching</u>.
When I was a son with my father,
Tender, the only one in the sight of my mother,
He taught me, and said to me,
"Let your heart hold fast my <u>words</u>;   *Heb.* davar, *Aram.* memra, *Gk.* logos
Keep my <u>commandments</u> and live."   *Decalogue:* deca: *ten* + logos: *word*

4:20-22   My son, be attentive to my <u>words</u>;
Incline your ear to my <u>sayings</u>.   *Heb.* emer *(pron.* aymer*)*
Let them not escape from your sight;
Keep them within your heart.   *"Thy word have I hid in my heart."*
For they are life to him who finds them,   *Ps. 119:11*
And healing to all his flesh.

6:20-23   My son, keep your father's <u>commandment</u>,
And forsake not your mother's <u>teaching</u>.
Bind them upon your heart always;   *ref. 3:3 (p. 45), 7:3 below*
Tie them about your neck.   *cf.* phylacteries
When you walk, they will lead you;
When you lie down, they will watch over you;
And when you awake, they will talk with you.
For the <u>commandment</u> is a lamp and the <u>teaching</u> is a light,
And the reproofs of discipline are the way of life.

7:1-3   My son, keep my <u>words</u>
          And treasure up my <u>commandments</u> with you.
          Keep my <u>commandments</u>, and live;
          Keep my <u>teachings</u> as the apple of your eye.   *"apple": pupil*
          Bind them on your fingers;   *cf.* phylacteries *(Deut. 6:8)*
          Write them on the tablet of your heart.   *ref. 3:3 (p. 45)*

13:13   He who despises the <u>word</u> brings destruction on himself,
          But he who respects the <u>commandment</u> will be rewarded.

19:16   He who keeps the <u>commandment</u> keeps his life;
          He who despises the <u>word</u> will die.

28:4   Those who forsake the <u>law</u> praise the wicked,   *ref. 25:26 (p. 64)*
          But those who keep the <u>law</u> strive against them.

28:7   He who keeps the <u>law</u> is a wise son,
          But a companion of gluttons shames his father.

28:9   If one turns away his ear from hearing the <u>law</u>,   *ref. 15:29 (p. 37)*
          Even his prayer is an abomination.   *God ignores sinners.*
                                                                      cf. Rom. 5:8

(See illustration, p. 34.)

29:18   Where there is no prophecy, the people cast off restraint,
          But blessed is he who keeps the <u>law</u>.

30:5-6   Every <u>word</u> of God proves true;   *Heb.* davar, *Aram.* memra, *Gk.* logos
          He is a shield to those who take refuge in Him.
          Do not add to His <u>words</u>,
          Lest He rebuke you, and you be found a liar.   *ref. Rev. 22:18,19*

LITIGATION

6:1-5   My son, if you have become surety for your neighbor,   *co-signing:*
           Have given your pledge for a stranger,   *bad business*
           If you are snared in the utterance of your lips,
           Caught in the words of your mouth,
           Then do this, my son, and save yourself,
           For you have come into your neighbor's power:
           Go, hasten, and importune your neighbor.
           Give your eyes no sleep
           And your eyelids no slumber;
           Save yourself like a gazelle from the hunter,
           Like a bird from the hand of the fowler.

11:14   Where there is no guidance, a people falls,
           But in an abundance of counselors there is safety.   *ref. 20:18 (p. 29)*

15:22   Without counsel plans go wrong,
           But with many advisors they succeed.

17:23   A wicked man accepts a bribe from the bosom   *ref. 15:27 (p. 53)*
           To pervert the ways of justice.

24:23b-26 Partiality in judging is not good.   *ref. 18:17 (p. 38)*
           He who says to the wicked, "You are innocent,"   *Gen. 18:25b*
           Will be cursed by peoples, abhorred by nations,
           But those who rebuke the wicked will have delight,
           And a good blessing will be upon them.
           He who gives a right answer kisses the lips.   *ref. 15:23 (p. 32)*

24:28   Be not a witness against your neighbor without cause,   *ref. 26:2 (p. 40)*
           And do not deceive with your lips.

MERCY, BROTHERHOOD, AND ALMS

3:3   Let not loyalty and faithfulness forsake you;
Bind them about your neck;   *ref. 6:21 and 7:3 (pp. 42, 43)*
Write them on the tablet of your heart.   *cf.* phylacteries, *Deut. 6:8, Jer. 31:33*

**By justice a king gives stability to the land.
(Prov. 29:4)**

3:27-28   Do not withhold good from those to whom it is due,
          … when it is in your power to do it.
          Do not say to your neighbor, "Go, and come again.   *pay wages on time*
          Tomorrow I will give it" — when you have it with you.   *Lev. 19:13*

11:17   A man who is kind benefits himself,
          But a cruel man hurts himself.

12:10   A righteous man has regard for the life of his beast,
          But the mercy of the wicked is cruel.   *cruelty to animals*

12:25   Anxiety in a man's heart weighs him down,   *rebukes versus*
          But a good word makes him glad.   *commendations*

13:23   The fallow ground of the <u>poor</u> yields much food,   *gleaning a portion*
          But it is swept away through injustice.   *vs. total harvesting*

14:10   The heart knows its own bitterness,   *Each person has private emotions*
          And no stranger shares its joy.   *known only by God.*

14:21-22 He who despises his neighbor is a sinner,
          But happy is he who is kind to the <u>poor</u>.
          Do they not err that devise evil?
          Those who devise good meet loyalty and faithfulness.

14:31   He who oppresses a <u>poor man</u> insults his Maker,   *ref. 22:22 (p. 18)*
          But he who is kind to the needy honors Him.   *ref. 17:5 below*

16:6   By loyalty and faithfulness iniquity is atoned for,
          And by the fear of Yahweh a man avoids evil.

17:5   He who mocks the <u>poor</u> insults his Maker;
          He who is glad at calamity will not go unpunished.   *Schadenfreude*

17:8-9   A <u>bribe</u> is like a magic stone in the eyes of him who gives it;
          Wherever he turns he <u>prospers</u>.   *reward of dishonesty, ref. 15:27 (p. 53)*
          He who forgives an offense seeks love,
          But he who repeats a matter alienates a friend.   *ref. 20:19 (p. 22)*

He who oppresses a poor man insults his Maker.
(Prov. 14:31)

17:17   A friend loves at all times,   *1 Cor. 13*
         And a brother is born for adversity.

18:16   A man's <u>gift</u> makes room for him   *ref. 17:8 above*
         And brings him before great men.

18:24   There are friends who pretend to be friends,
         But there is a friend who sticks closer than a brother.

19:6   Many seek the favor of a generous man,   *golden rings given by Norse kings*
         And everyone is a friend to a man who gives <u>gifts</u>.   *ref. 18:16 above*

19:17   He who is kind to the <u>poor</u> lends to Yahweh,   *lay up treasure*
         And He will repay him for his deed.   *in heaven*

20:6   Many a man proclaims his own loyalty,
         But a faithful man who can find?   *cf. Diogenes and his lamp*

21:10   The soul of the wicked desires evil;
         His neighbor finds no mercy in his eyes.

21:13-14 He who closes his ear to the cry of the <u>poor</u>
         will himself cry out and not be heard.
         A <u>gift</u> in secret averts anger,   *ref. 17:8 above*
         and a <u>bribe</u> in the bosom, strong wrath.

22:9   He who has a bountiful eye will be blessed,
         For he shares his bread with the <u>poor</u>.

24:10-12 If you faint in the day of adversity, your strength is small.
         Rescue those who are being taken away to death;   *cf. Schindler and*
         Hold back those who are stumbling to the slaughter.   *"righteous Gentiles"*
         If you say, "Behold, we did not know this,"
         Does not He who weighs the heart perceive it?   *cf. Egyptian judgment scales*
         Does not He who keeps watch over your soul know it,   *Watchers, Dan. 4:13*
         And will He not requite man according to his work?   *books in Rev. 20:12*

24:29   Do not say, "I will do to him as he has done to me;   *negative Golden Rule*
         I will pay the man back for what he has done."

25:9-10 Argue your case with your neighbor himself,
And do not disclose another's secret,
Lest he who hears you bring shame upon you
And your ill repute have no end.

25:21-22 If your enemy is hungry, give him bread to eat,
And if he is thirsty, give him water to drink,
For you will heap coals of fire on his head,   *Rom. 12:20*
And Yahweh will reward you.

27:9-10 Oil and perfume make the heart glad,   *anointing a sign of favor*
But the soul is torn by trouble.   *Ps. 104:15*
Your friend, and your father's friend, do not forsake,
And do not go to your brother's house in the day of your calamity.
Better is a neighbor who is near
Than a brother who is far away.

27:17 Iron sharpens iron   *progress through conflict*
And one man sharpens another.   *and competition*

27:19 As in water face answers to face,   *ref. 23:7 (p. 55) alternate reading*
So the mind of man reflects man.   *You are what you think.*

27:21 The crucible is for silver, and the furnace is for gold,   *1 Cor. 3:12-13*
And a man is judged by his praise.   *Flattery is a furnace to try pride.*

28:27 He who gives to the <u>poor</u> will not want,
But he who hides his eyes will get many a curse.

29:13 The <u>poor man</u> and the oppressor meet together;   *ref. 22:2 (p. 54)*
Yahweh gives light to the eyes of both.   *Matt. 5:45, "Rain falls on all men."*

PRIDE

11:2   When pride comes, then comes disgrace,   *pride the sin of Satan/Adam*
                But with the humble is wisdom.   *Isa. 14:13*

13:10   By insolence the heedless make strife,
                But with those who take advice is wisdom.

14:3   The talk of a fool is a rod for his back (or a rod of pride),
                But the lips of the wise will preserve them.

15:25   Yahweh tears down the house of the proud
                But maintains the widow's boundaries.   *ref. 23:10 (p. 55)*

16:5   Everyone who is arrogant is an abomination to Yahweh;   *hubris*
                Be assured, he will not go unpunished.

16:18-19   Pride goes before destruction   *Conceit brings defeat.*
                And a haughty spirit before a fall.   *hubris*
                It is better to be of a lowly spirit with the poor
                Than to divide the spoil with the proud.

18:11-12   A rich man's wealth is his strong city   *ref. 10:15 (p. 52)*
                And like a high wall protecting him (in his imagination).
                Before destruction a man's heart is haughty,
                But humility goes before honor.

21:4   Haughty eyes and a proud heart,
                The lamp of the wicked, are sin.

21:24   "Scoffer" is the name of the proud, haughty man
                who acts with arrogant pride.   *"scoffer": Heb.* letz *(p. 96)*

26:12   Do you see a man who is wise in his own eyes?   *ref. 3:7 (p. 75)*
                There is more hope for a fool than for him.

27:2   Let another praise you and not your own mouth,
        A stranger and not your own lips.

28:11   A rich man is wise in his own eyes,   *ref. 3:7 (p. 75)*
        But a poor man who has understanding will find him out.

28:25   A greedy man stirs up strife,
        But he who trusts in Yahweh will be enriched.

29:23   A man's pride will bring him low,
        But he who is lowly in spirit will obtain honor.

30:13   There are those - how lofty are their eyes,
        How high their eyebrows lift!

30:21-23 Under three things the earth trembles;   *Examples:*
          Under four it cannot bear up: *Eugene O'Neill's*
          A slave when he becomes king, and   *Emperor Jones*
          A fool when he is filled with food,   *Shakespeare's "Falstaff"*
          An unloved woman when she gets a husband, and   *Bloody Mary*
          A maid when she succeeds her mistress.   *Sarah and Hagar*

30:32   If you have been foolish, exalting yourself,
        Or if you have been devising evil,
        Put your hand on your mouth.   *curb your appetite*

52

PROSPERITY AND BUSINESS

| 10:15 | A rich man's wealth is his strong city;
The poverty of the poor is their ruin. | *ref. 18:11 (p. 50)*
Jewish materialism: money talks
Mammon is good. |

| 10:22 | The blessing of <u>Yahweh makes rich</u>,
And He adds no sorrow with it. | *divine bias*
ref. 28:21 (p. 41) |

| 11:15-16 | He who gives <u>surety</u> for a stranger will smart for it,
But he sho hates suretyship is secure.
A gracious woman gets honor,
And violent men get riches. | *Co-signing on a loan is bad.*

Pillaging pays. |

| 11:24-26 | One man gives freely, yet grows all the richer;
Another withholds what he should give and only suffers want.
A liberal man will be enriched,
And one who waters will himself be watered.
The people curse him who holds back grain,
But a blessing is on the head of him who sells it. | *Charity pays.*

hoarded food in famine
price gouging swindle
black market profits |

| 12:9 | Better is a man of humble standing who works for himself
Than one who plays the great man but lacks bread. | *private enterprise* |

| 13:7-8 | One man pretends to be rich, yet has nothing;
Another pretends to be poor, yet has great wealth.
The <u>ransom</u> of a man's life is his wealth,
But a poor man has no means of <u>redemption</u>. | |

| 13:18 | Poverty and disgrace come to him who ignores instruction,
But he who heeds reproof is honored. | |

| 13:22 | A good man leaves an inheritance to his children's children,
But the sinner's wealth is laid up for the righteous. | *progeny*
prosperity |

13:25   The righteous has enough to satisfy his appetite,
          But the belly of the wicked suffers want.

14:4   Where there are no oxen, there is no grain.   *status symbols: horse and ox:*
         But abundant crops come by the strength of the ox.   *for warrior, farmer*

14:19-20   The evil bow down before the good,   *contradictions*
         The wicked at the gates of the righteous.
         The <u>poor</u> is disliked even by his neighbor,   *ref. 19:7 (p. 54)*
         But the rich has many friends.

14:24   The crown of the wise is their wisdom (or riches),   *ref. 13:18 (p. 81)*
         But folly is the <u>garland</u> of fools.   *ref. 4:9 (p. 76)*

14:28   In a multitude of people is the glory of a king,   *cf. David's census,*
         But without people a prince is ruined.   *2 Sam. 24:1*

14:35   A servant who deals wisely has the king's favor,
         But his wrath falls on one who acts shamefully.

15:6   In the house of the righteous there is much treasure,
         But trouble befalls the income of the wicked.

15:16-17   Better is a little with the fear of Yahweh
         Than great treasure and trouble with it.
         Better is a dinner of herbs where love is
         Than a fatted ox and hatred with it.

15:27   He who is greedy for unjust gain makes trouble for his household,
         But he who hates <u>bribes</u> will live.   *ref. 17:23 (p. 44),*
                 17:8 (p. 46), 18:16 (p. 48), 21:14 (p. 48)
                        1 Sam. 8:3, Ps. 26:10, Isa. 33:15

16:8   Better is a little with righteousness
         Than great revenues with injustice.

17:18   A man without sense gives a pledge,   *ref. 11:15 (p. 52)*
         And becomes <u>surety</u> in the presence of his neighbor.

18:9   He who is slack in his work   *Unearned wages equal*
           Is a brother to him who destroys.   *payment for clumsy damages.*

18:23   The poor use entreaties,   *begging poor*
           But the rich answer roughly.   *hardhearted rich*

19:4   Wealth brings many new friends,
           But a poor man is deserted by his friend.

19:7   All a poor man's brothers hate him;
           How much more do his friends go far from him!

20:14   "It is bad; it is bad," says the buyer,   *caveat emptor*
           But when he goes away, then he boasts.   *"ballyhoo" of the Arabic bazaar*

20:16   Take a man's garment when he has given surety for a stranger,
           And hold him in pledge when he gives surety for foreigners.   *ref. 27:13*
                                                      (p. 57)

20:21   An inheritance gotten hastily in the beginning   *parvenu riche*
           Will in the end not be blessed.

21:17   He who loves pleasure will be a poor man;
           He who loves wine and oil will not be rich.   *ref. 23:20 (p. 71)*

22:1-2   A good name is to be chosen rather than great riches,
           And favor is better than silver or gold.   *ref. 29:13 (p. 49)*
           The rich and the poor meet together;   *determinism: Isa. 45:7,*
           Yahweh is the Maker of them all.   *Deut. 32:39, Amos 3:6*

22:4   The reward for humility and fear of Yahweh   *Controller of fortune*
           is riches and honor and life.   *ref. 17:6 (p. 38), Exod. 20:12*
                    (Existential rewards: prosperity, dignity, longevity)

22:7   The rich rules over the poor,   *poverty accepted*
           And the borrower is the slave of the lender.   *slavery accepted*

22:16   He who oppresses the poor to increase his own wealth
           or gives to the rich will only come to want.

22:26-29   Be not one of those who give pledges,
          Who become <u>surety</u> for debts.
          If you have nothing with which to pay,
          Why should your bed be taken from under you?

          Remove not the ancient landmark   *boundaries sacred*
          Which your fathers have set.   *ref. 23:10*

          Do you see a man skilful in his work?
          He will stand before kings;
          He will not stand before obscure men.

23:1-8   When you sit down to eat with a ruler,   *cf.* "Proverbs from
          Observe carefully what is before you;   Egypt" *(p. 102)*
          And put a knife to your throat
          If you are a man given to appetite.
          Do not desire his delicacies,
          For they are deceptive food.
          Do not toil to acquire wealth;
          Be wise enough to desist.
          When your eyes light upon it, it is gone,
          For suddenly it takes to itself wings,
          Flying like an eagle toward heaven.
          Do not eat the bread of a man who is stingy;
          Do not desire his delicacies;
          For he is like one who is inwardly reckoning.
                  (Alternate: "For as he thinketh in his heart, so is he.")
          "Eat and drink!" he says to you,
          But his heart is not with you.
          You will vomit the morsels which you have eaten
          And waste your pleasant words.

23:10-11 Do not remove an ancient landmark   *boundaries sacred*
          Or enter the fields of the fatherless;   *ref. 15:25 (p. 50)*
          For their <u>Redeemer</u> is strong;   *Heb.* go'el: *kinsman rescuer*
          He will plead their cause against you.

24:27   Prepare your work outside;
          Get everything ready for you in the field,
          And after that build your house.

25:16   If you have found <u>honey</u>, eat only enough for you,
        Lest you be sated with it and vomit it.

25:25   Like cold water to a thirsty soul,
        So is good news from a far country.

25:27   It is not good to eat much <u>honey</u>,
        So be sparing of complimentary words.

Remove not the ancient landmark
Which your fathers have set.
(Prov. 22:28, 23:10)
(See also depiction of the
ancient cosmos, p. 26.)

ATKINS

27:7-8   He who is sated loathes <u>honey</u>,
           But to one who is hungry everything bitter is sweet.
           Like a bird that strays from its nest,
           Is a man who strays from his home.

27:13   Take a man's garment when he has given <u>surety</u> for a stranger
           And hold him in pledge when he gives <u>surety</u> for foreigners. *ref. 20:16 (p. 54)*

27:18   He who tends a fig tree will eat its fruit,   *ref. 12:11 (p. 66)*
           And he who guards his master will be honored.

27:23-27   Know well the condition of your flocks,   *sound business advice*
           And give attention to your herds;
           For riches do not last forever,
           And does a crown endure to all generations?
           When the grass is gone and the new growth appears
           And the herbage of the mountains is gathered,
           The lambs will provide your clothing
           And the goats the price of a field;
           There will be enough goats' milk for your food,
           For the good of your household
           And maintenance for your maidens.

28:3   A <u>poor man</u> who oppresses the poor is a beating rain that leaves no food.

28:20   A <u>faithful man</u> will abound with blessings,
           But he who hastens to be rich will not go unpunished.

28:22   A <u>miserly man</u> hastens after wealth
           And does not know that want will come upon him.

30:10   Do not slander a servant to his master,
           Lest he curse you and you be held guilty.   *potency of cursing*

30:14   There are those whose teeth are swords,
           Whose teeth are knives,
           To devour the <u>poor</u> from off the earth,
           The needy from among men.   2nd Thesalanians

RIGHTEOUSNESS

Heb. tsedeq (zedek)

(*derivatives: Zadokites, Zedekiah, Melchizedek*)

JUDUHISM
- Rule Keeping
- Commandments
- Kept their vc
- Works Religion
- Auto Soteria

2:12-15 ... delivering you from the way of evil,
From men of perverted speech,
Who forsake the paths of <u>uprightness</u>   *Heb.* yosher (Jasher)
To walk in the ways of darkness,
Who rejoice in doing evil
And delight in the perverseness of evil;
Men whose paths are crooked,
And who are devious in their ways.

2:20-22 So you will walk in the way of good men
And keep to the paths of the <u>righteous</u>.   *Heb.* tsadiq
For the <u>upright</u> will inhabit the land,   *Heb.* yashar (Jasher)
The men of integrity will remain in it,   *"Meek will inherit ..." (Matt. 5:5)*
But the wicked will be cut off from the land,
And the treacherous will be rooted out of it.

3:33-34 Yahweh's <u>curse</u> is on the house of the wicked,   *Yahweh's malediction like*
But He blesses the abode of the righteous.   *a sorcerer-conjurer (Balaam)*
Toward the <u>scorners</u> He is scornful,   *"scorner": Heb.* letz (p. 96)
But to the humble He shows favor.

4:14-19 Do not enter the path of the wicked,
And do not walk in the way of evil men.
Avoid it; do not go on it;
Turn away from it and pass on.
For they cannot sleep unless they have done wrong;
They are robbed of sleep unless they have made someone stumble.
For they eat the bread of wickedness
And drink the wine of violence.   *cf. God's wine of wrath (Rev. 14:10)*
But the path of the righteous is like the light of dawn,
Which shines brighter and brighter until full day.
The way of the wicked is like deep darkness;
They do not know over what they stumble.

The wicked will be cut off from the land.
(Prov. 2:22)

4:23-27	Keep your <u>heart</u> with all vigilance,	*keep the whole body pure*
	For from it flow the springs of life.	
	Put away from you crooked <u>speech</u>,	*sins of the whole body*
	And put devious <u>talk</u> far from you.	
	Let your <u>eyes</u> look directly forward,	
	And your gaze be straight before you.	
	Take heed to the path of your <u>feet</u>;	
	Then all your ways will be sure.	
	Do not swerve to the right or to the left;	
	Turn your <u>foot</u> away from evil.	
6:16-19	There are six things which Yahweh hates,	
	Seven which are an abomination to Him:	*Seven Sins:*
	Haughty eyes,	*pride*
	A lying tongue, and	*dishonesty*
	Hands that shed innocent blood	*murder*
	A heart that devises wicked plans,	*intrigue*
	Feet that make haste to run to evil,	*perversity*
	A false witness who breathes out lies, and	*perjury*
	A man who sows discord among brothers.	*brawling*
10:2-3	Treasures gained by wickedness do not profit,	
	But righteousness delivers from death.	*Matt. 5:6 vs. Luke 6:21*
	Yahweh does not let the righteous go hungry,	*divine bias*
	But He thwarts the craving of the wicked.	*ref. 28:19 (p. 69)*
10:9	He who walks in integrity walks securely,	
	But he who perverts his ways will be found out.	
10:11	The mouth of the righteous is a <u>Fountain of Life</u>,	*ref. 14:27 (p. 1)*
	But the mouth of the wicked conceals violence.	
10:16	The wage of the righteous leads to life,	*"The wages of sin is death."*
	The gain of the wicked to sin.	*(Rom. 6:23)*
10:23-25	It is like sport to a <u>fool</u> to do wrong,	*"fool": Heb. kesil (p. 96)*
	But wise conduct is pleasure to a man of understanding.	
	What the wicked dreads will come upon him,	
	But the desire of the righteous will be granted.	

When the tempest passes, the wicked is no more,
But the righteous is established forever.   *house on a rock (Matt. 7:24)*

11:3-8   The integrity of the upright guides them,   *cf. "Do not be too good ..."*
          But the crookedness of the treacherous destroys them.   *Eccl. 7:16-17*
          Riches do not profit in the day of wrath,   *Amos 5:18, Zeph. 1:14*
          But righteousness delivers from death.
          The righteousness of the blameless keeps his way straight,   *KJV "perfect":*
          But the wicked falls by his own wickedness.   *Heb.* tamiym
          The righteousness of the upright delivers them,
          But the treacherous are taken captive by their lust.
          When the wicked dies, his hope perishes,   *Isa. 66:24, Dan. 12:2*
          And the expectation of the godless comes to nought.
          The righteous is delivered from trouble,
          And the wicked gets into it instead.

11:28   He who trusts in his riches will wither,
          But the righteous will flourish like a green leaf.

11:30   The fruit of the righteous is a Tree of Life,   *ref. 15:4 (p. 21)*
          But lawlessness takes away lives.   *longevity, not immortality, in O.T.*

12:2-3   A good man obtains favor from Yahweh,
          But a man of evil devices He condemns.   *God curses*
          A man is not established by wickedness,
          But the root of the righteous will never be moved.

12:26   A righteous man turns away from evil,
          But the way of the wicked leads them astray.

12:28   In the path of righteousness is life,   *existentialism:*
          But the way of error leads to death.   *long life versus short life*

13:6   Righteousness guards him whose way is upright,
          But sin overthrows the wicked.

14:2   He who walks in uprightness fears Yahweh,
          But he who is devious in his ways despises Him.   *Sinners hate God.*

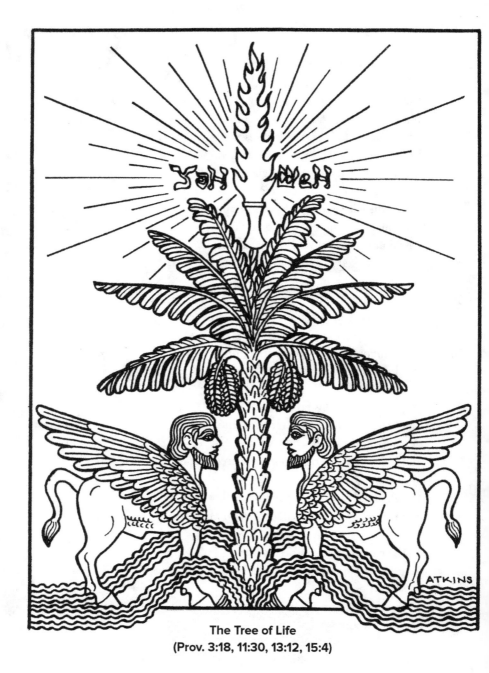

The Tree of Life
(Prov. 3:18, 11:30, 13:12, 15:4)

The Fountain of Life
(Prov. 13:14, 16:22, 14:27)

14:9   God scorns the wicked,   *God hates sinners.*
           But the upright enjoy His favor.

14:16   A wise man is cautious and turns away from evil,
           But a fool throws off restraint and is careless.   *devil-may-care conduct*

14:34   Righteousness exalts a nation,   *corporate favor*
           But sin is a reproach to any people.   *corporate guilt*

15:26   The thoughts of the wicked are an abomination to Yahweh; *ref. 11:18-21 (p. 35)*
           The words of the pure are pleasing to Him.   *15:8-12 (p. 37)*

15:28   The <u>mind</u> of the righteous ponders how to answer,
           But the <u>mouth</u> of the wicked pours out evil things.   *ref. 15:2 (p. 81),*
                                                              James 3:6

16:6   By loyalty and faithfulness iniquity is atoned for,   *faithful pardoned*
           And by the fear of Yahweh a man avoids evil.

16:17   The highway of the upright turns aside from evil;
           He who guards his way preserves his <u>life</u>.   *long life, not immortality*

16:31   A hoary head is a crown of glory;   *the elder, the patriarch, esteemed*
           It is gained in a righteous life.   *elder: Heb. zaqen, Gk. presbyteros*

18:10   The <u>Name of Yahweh</u> is a strong tower;   *The Name: Heb.* Ha Shem
           The righteous man runs into it and is safe.   ~~*Micah 4:5*~~

19:23   The <u>fear of Yahweh</u> leads to <u>life</u>;   *long life: "a hoary head" (16:31)*
           And he who has it rests satisfied;
           He will not be visited by <u>harm</u>.

                                             11. 7~8
                                           12. 28

20:7   A righteous man who walks in his integrity —
           Blessed are his sons after him!   *blessing passes to future generations*

20:9   Who can say, "I have made my heart clean;   *Noah perfect (Gen. 6:9)*
           I am pure from my sin?"   *only if the conscience is seared.*

20:11   Even a child makes himself known by his acts,
           Whether what he does is pure and right.

21:2   Every way of a man is right in his own eyes,   *ref. 30:12 (p. 65), 16:2 (p. 37)*
        But Yahweh weighs the heart.   *Judges 21:25: need for Law*
                                                         cf. Egyptian Judgment of the Dead with Scales

21:8   The way of the guilty is crooked,
        But the conduct of the pure is <u>right</u>.   *straight*

21:21   He who pursues <u>righteousness</u> and <u>kindness</u>   *ref. Matt. 5:6*
        Will find <u>life</u> and <u>honor</u>.   *rewards: long life and fame*

21:29   A wicked man puts on a bold face,
        But an upright man considers his ways.

                                         covet
23:17-18 Let not your heart (envy) sinners,   *ref. 24:1 (p. 24)*
          But continue in the fear of Yahweh all the day.
          Surely there is a <u>future</u>,   *longevity, not immortality*
          And your <u>hope</u> will not be cut off.   *hope for reward, not heaven*

23:24-25 The father of the righteous will greatly rejoice;
          He who begets a wise son will be glad in him.
          Let your father and mother be glad;
          Let her who bore you rejoice.

24:15   Lie not in wait as a wicked man   *house-breaking*
        against the dwelling of the righteous;   *a capital crime*
        Do not violence to his home.

25:26   Like a muddied spring or a poluted fountain   *ref. 28:4 (p. 43)*
        Is a righteous man who gives way before the wicked.
                                 Enigma: resist not evil (Matt. 5:39). Resist the Devil (Jas. 4:7)

28:1   The wicked flee when no one pursues,   *ref. 22:13 (p. 67)*
        But the righteous are bold as a lion.   *1 Pet. 5:8 (Devil a lion)*

28:6   Better is a poor man who walks in his integrity   *blessed are the poor (in spirit)*
        Than a rich man who is perverse in his ways.

28:12-14 When the righteous triumph, there is great glory,
          But when the wicked rise, men hide themselves.

He who conceals his transgressions will not prosper.
But he who confesses and forsakes them will obtain mercy.
<u>Blessed</u> is the man who fears Yahweh always,   *Old Testament beatitude*
But he who hardens his heart will fall into calamity.   *Free will: rebellion*

28:18   He who walks in integrity will be delivered,
         But he who is perverse in his ways will fall into a pit.

28:28   When the wicked rise, men hide themselves,   *ref. 28:12 above*
         But when they perish, the righteous increase.

29:2   When the righteous are in authority, the people rejoice,
         But when the wicked rule, the people groan.   *Bad government (p. 29)*

29:6-7   An evil man is ensnared in his transgression,
         But a righteous man sings and rejoices.
         A righteous man knows the rights of the poor;   *human rights*
         A wicked man does not understand such knowledge.

29:10   Bloodthirsty men hate one who is blameless,   *The World vs. Christ*
         And the wicked seek his life.   *vs. martyrs (Heb. 11:38).*

29:16   When the wicked are in authority, transgression increases,   *ref. 29:2 above*
         But the righteous will look upon their downfall.

29:27   An unjust man is an abomination to the righteous,
         But he whose way is straight is an abomination to the wicked.

30:12   There are those who are pure in their own eyes   *ref. 21:2 (p. 64)*
         but are not cleansed of their filth.

SLOTH AND WASTE

6:6-9 Go to the ant, O <u>sluggard</u>;   *Heb.* atsel: *slothful (p. 96)*
     Consider her ways and be wise.   *John 6:12*
     Without having any chief, officer, or ruler, *"Let nothing be wasted."*
     She prepares her food in summer,
     And gathers her sustenance in harvest.
     How long will you lie there, O <u>sluggard</u>?
     When will you rise from your sleep?

6:10-11 A little sleep, a little slumber,   *ref. 24:33 (p. 69)*
     A little folding of the hands to rest,
     And poverty will come upon you like a vagabond,
     And want like an armed man.

10:4-5 A slack hand causes poverty,
     But the hand of the diligent makes rich.
     A son who gathers in summer is prudent,
     But a son who sleeps in harvest brings shame.

10:26 Like vinegar to the teeth and smoke to the eyes,
     So is the <u>sluggard</u> to those who send him.

               First priority: Put food on the table.
12:11 He who tills his land will have plenty of bread, *ref. 28:19 (p. 69)*
     But he who follows worthless pursuits has no sense. *work before hobbies*

12:24 The hand of the diligent will rule,
     While the slothful will be put to forced labor. *slavery accepted*

12:27 A slothful man will not catch his prey,
     But the diligent man will get precious wealth.

13:4 The soul of the <u>sluggard</u> craves and gets nothing,
     While the soul of the diligent is richly supplied.

13:11   Wealth hastily gotten will dwindle,   *"A penny saved is a penny earned."*
         But he who gathers little by little will increase it.

                                    Scottish saying: "Mony a mickle makes a muckle."

14:23   In all toil there is profit,   *Sweat and elbow grease are productive.*
         But mere talk tends only to want.

15:19   The way of a <u>sluggard</u> is overgrown with thorns,
         But the path of the upright is a level highway.

16:26   A worker's appetite works for him;
         His mouth urges him on.

19:15   Slothfulness casts into a deep sleep,
         And an idle person will suffer hunger.

19:24   The <u>sluggard</u> buries his hand in the dish,
         And will not even bring it back to his mouth.

20:4   The <u>sluggard</u> does not plow in the autumn;
         He will seek at harvest and have nothing.

20:13   Love not sleep, lest you come to poverty;
         Open your eyes, and you will have plenty of bread.

21:5   The plans of the diligent lead surely to abundance,
         But everyone who is hasty comes only to want.

21:25-26 The desire of the <u>sluggard</u> kills him,
         For his hands refuse to labor.
         All day long the wicked covets,
         But the righteous gives and does not hold back

22:13   The <u>sluggard</u> says, "There is a lion outside!"   *false fear of enterprise*
         I shall be slain in the streets!"   *The one-talent man hides his talent.*

He who tills the land will have plenty of bread.
(Prov. 12:11, 28:19)

24:30-32 I passed by the field of a <u>sluggard</u>,   *Heb.* atsel: *slothful (p. 96)*
             By the vineyard of a man without sense,
             And, lo, it was all overgrown with thorns;
             The ground was covered with nettles,
             And its stone wall was broken down.
             Then I saw and considered it;
             I looked and received instruction.

24:33-34 A little sleep, a little slumber,   *ref. 6:10 (p. 66)*
             A little folding of the hands to rest,
             And poverty will come upon you like a robber,
             And want like an armed man.

25:17   Let your foot be seldom in your neighbor's house,
             Lest he become weary of you and hate you.   *Do not wear out your welcome.*

26: 13-16 The <u>sluggard</u> says, "There is a lion in the road!
             There is a lion in the streets!"
             As a door turns on its hinges,
             So does a <u>sluggard</u> on his bed.
             The <u>sluggard</u> buries his hand in the dish;
             It wears him out to bring it back to his mouth.
             The <u>sluggard</u> is wiser in his own eyes
             Than seven men who can answer discreetly.

28:19   He who tills his land will have plenty of bread,   *ref. 12:11 (p. 66)*
             But he who follows worthless pursuits will have plenty of poverty.

TITHES AND OFFERINGS

3:9-10   Honor Yahweh with your substance
And with the firstfruits of all your produce.
Then your barns will be filled with plenty
And your vats will be bursting with wine.

21:27   The sacrifice of the wicked is an abomination;   *ref. 15:8 (p. 37)*
How much more when he brings it with evil intent.   *21:3 (p. 39)*

Luke 7:34
MATTH 11:19
John 2:9
MATTH 9:17
1ST TIMOTHY 5:23

WINE

20:1   Wine is a <u>mocker</u>;

Strong drink a brawler,

And whoever is led astray by it is not wise.

"mocker": Heb. letz (p. 96)

Nazirite vow: Num. 6:1-8

John the Baptist: Luke 1:15

23:20-21   Be not among winebibbers

Or among gluttonous eaters of meat,

For the drunkard and the glutton will come to poverty,

And drowsiness will clothe a man with rags.

Rechabite vow: Jer. 35:2, 5-7,14

Acts 21:23-24, 23:12

ref. 21:17 (p. 54)

23:29-35   Who has woe? Who has sorrow?

Who has strife? Who has complaining?

Who has wounds without cause?

Who has redness of eyes?

Those who tarry long over wine;

Those who go to try mixed wine.

Do not look at wine when it is red,

When it sparkles in the cup and goes down smoothly.

At the last it bites like a serpent

And stings like an adder.

Your eyes will see strange things

And your mind utter perverse things.

You will be like one who lies down in the midst of the sea,

Like one who lies on the top of a mast.

"They struck me," you will say, "but I was not hurt;

They beat me, but I did not feel it.

When shall I awake? I will seek another drink."

Eph. 5:18, Acts 2:12-15

cocktails

31:4-5   It is not for kings, O Lemuel,

It is not for kings to drink wine or for rulers to desire strong drink,

Lest they drink and forget what has been decreed

And pervert the rights of all the afflicted.

31:6-7   Give strong drink to him who is perishing   *wine for cheer*
           And wine to those in bitter distress.   *Ps. 104:15, Deut. 14:26*
           Let them drink and forget their poverty   *Song of Sol. 4:10*
           And remember their misery no more.

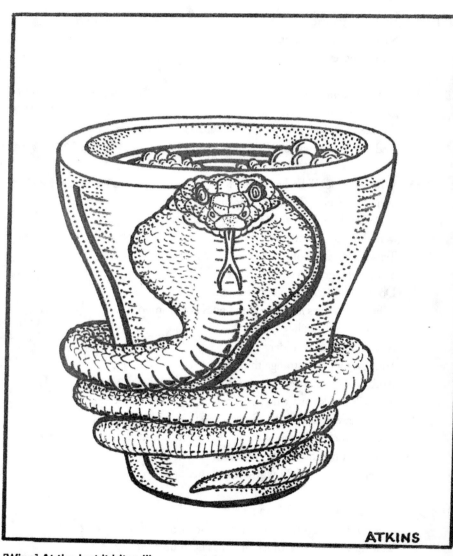

ATKINS

[Wine] At the last it bites like a serpent
And stings like an adder.
(Prov. 23:32)

WISDOM

1:2-7   That men may know <u>wisdom</u> and <u>instruction</u>,   *Heb.* hokmah *and* musar:
         Understand words of insight,   *discipline, chastisement*
         Receive instruction in wise dealing, righteousness,
         justice, and equity;
         That prudence may be given to the simple,
         Knowledge and discretion to the youth -
         The wise man also may hear and increase in learning,
         And the man of <u>understanding</u> acquire skill,   *Heb.* binah: *reason*
         To understand a proverb and a figure,
         The words of the wise and their riddles.
         The fear of Yahweh is the beginning of <u>knowledge</u>;   *Heb.* da'ath
         Fools despise wisdom and instruction.

1:20-33   Wisdom cries aloud in the street;   *Wisdom personified, a goddess*
         In the markets she raises her voice;   —*not by Solomon, later influence of*
         On the top of the walls she cries out;   *post-captivity Zoroastrianism*
         At the entrance of the city gates she speaks: *cf. Folly, 9:13 (p. 15)*
         "How long, O simple ones, will you love being simple?
         How long will scoffers delight in their scoffing
         and fools hate knowledge?
         Give heed to my reproof;
         Behold, I will pour out my thoughts to you;
         I will make my words known to you.
         Because I have called and you refused to listen,
         Have stretched out my hand and no one has heeded,
         And you have ignored all my counsel
         And would have none of my reproof,
         I also will laugh at your calamity;   *Schadenfreude: ridicule of enemies*
         I will mock when panic strikes you,   *ref. 24:17 (p. 40), Ps. 23:5*
         When panic strikes you like a storm,   *tempest*
         And your calamity comes like a whirlwind,   *tornado, Typhon*
         When distress and anguish come upon you.
         Then they will call upon me, but I will not answer;   *too late for the*
         They will <u>seek me</u> diligently but will not find me.   *hard-hearted sinner*
                                                 "Seek ye the LORD."

Because they hated knowledge
And did not choose the fear of Yahweh,   *Isa. 55:6*
Would have none of my counsel,
And despised all my reproof,
Therefore they shall eat the fruit of their way
And be sated with their own devices.
For the simple are killed by their turning away,
And the complacence of fools destroys them;
But he who listens to me will dwell secure
And will be at ease, without dread of evil."

2:1-11   My son, if you receive my words
And treasure up my commandments with you,   *Sephiroth of Kabbala:*
Making your ear attentive to <u>wisdom</u>   Hokmah
And inclining your heart to <u>understanding</u>;   Binah
Yes, if you cry out for <u>insight</u>   Da'ath (de'oth)
And raise your voice for understanding,
If you seek it like silver
And search for it as for hidden treasures,
Then you will understand the <u>fear</u> of Yahweh   Pachad
And find the knowledge of God.   *"fear of Isaac" (Gen. 31:42)*
For Yahweh gives wisdom;   *determinism: ref. Rom. 12:3*
From His mouth come knowledge and understanding;   *Emanations*
He stores up sound wisdom for the upright;
He is a shield to those who walk in integrity,
Guarding the paths of justice
And preserving the way of His saints.   *perseverance of saints*
Then you will understand righteousness and justice
and equity, every good path;
For wisdom will come from your heart,
And knowledge will be pleasant to your soul;
<u>Discretion</u> will watch over you;   *Heb. M'zimmah: sagacity, personified*
<u>Understanding</u> will guard you.   *Heb. T'bunah, reason, personified*

3:4-8   So you will find favor and good repute
In the sight of God and man.   *origin of Luke 2:52*
Trust in Yahweh with all your heart,
And <u>do not rely on your own insight</u>.   *anti-intellectualism: Gen. 2:17,*
In all your ways acknowledge Him,   *Deut. 29:29, Ps. 131:1, Eccl. 1:17-18*

And He will make straight your paths.

Do not be wise in your own eyes;   *ref. 12:15 (p.81), 16:2 (p.37), 21:2 (p.64),*

Fear Yahweh and turn away from evil.   *28:11 (p. 51), 30:12 (p. 65)*

It will be healing to your flesh

And refreshment to your <u>bones</u>.   *bones: bodily strength*

3:13-26   Happy is the man who finds wisdom,   *not "Wisdom"*

And the man who gets understanding,   *intelligence from: nature/nurture,*

For the gain from it is better than the gain from silver   *genes/upbringing,*

And its profit better than gold.   *heritage/environment*

She is more precious than jewels,   *personification passage inserted later*

And nothing you desire can compare with her.

Long life is in her right hand;   *verse claimed by palmists,*

In her left hand are riches and honor.   *chiromancers*

Her ways are ways of pleasantness,

And all her paths are peace.

She is a <u>Tree of Life</u> to those who lay hold of her;   *ref. 15:4 (p. 21)*

Those who hold her feet are called happy.   *See illustration, p. 77*

Yahweh by wisdom founded the earth;

By understanding He established the heavens;

By His knowledge the deeps broke forth,

And the clouds drop down the dew...

My son, keep sound wisdom and discretion;

Let them not escape from your sight,

And they will be <u>life</u> for your soul   *cf. Jewish "חי" (chai: life)*

And <u>adornment</u> for your neck.   *as ornament or necklace*

Then you will walk on your way securely,

And your foot will not stumble.   *ref. 4:12 (p. 76)*

If you sit down, you will not be afraid;

When you lie down your sleep will be sweet.

Do not be afraid of sudden panic,

Or of the ruin of the wicked when it comes;

For Yahweh will be your confidence

And will keep your foot from being caught.

3:35   The wise will inherit honor;
           But fools get disgrace.

4:5-13   Do not forget, and do not turn away from the words of my mouth.
           Get Wisdom; get Insight.
           Do not forsake her, and she will keep you;
           Love her, and she will guard you.
           The beginning of wisdom is this:
           Get Wisdom, and whatever you get,
           Get Insight.
           Prize her highly, and she will exalt you;
           She will honor you if you embrace her.
           She will place on your head a fair garland;   *ref. 14:18 (p. 81), 14:24 (p. 53)*
           She will bestow on you a beautiful crown.   *victor's laurel, Gk.* stephanos
           Hear, my son, and accept my words,
           That the years of your life may be many.
           I have taught you the way of wisdom;
           I have led you in the paths of uprightness.

           When you walk, your step will not be hampered;
           And if you run, you will not stumble.
           Keep hold of Instruction, do not let go;
           Guard her, for she is your life.

5:1-2   My son, be attentive to my wisdom;
           Incline your ear to my understanding,
           That you may keep discretion,
           And your lips may guard knowledge.

7:4   Say to Wisdom, "You are my sister,"
           And call Insight your intimate friend.

She will place on your head a fair garland.
(Prov. 4:9)

8:1-36   Does not Wisdom call;   *Wisdom: Heb. Hokmah, Gk. Sophia*
          Does not Understanding raise her voice?   *Gnostic Aeon: divine Emanation*
          On the heights beside the way,   *Mother of Logos (Messiah)*
          In the paths she takes her stand;   *Rev. 12:1-6*
          Beside the gates in front of the town,
          At the entrance of the portals she cries aloud:
          "To you, O men, I call,
          And my cry is to the sons of men.
          O simple ones, learn prudence;
          O foolish men, pay attention.
          Hear, for I will speak noble things,
          And from my lips will come what is right;
          For my mouth will utter truth;
          Wickedness is an abomination to my lips.
          All the words of my mouth are righteous;
          There is nothing crooked or twisted in them.
          They are all straight to him who understands
          And right to those who find knowledge.
          Take my instruction instead of silver,
          And knowledge rather than choice gold;
          For Wisdom is better than jewels,
          And all that you may desire cannot compare with her.
          I, Wisdom, dwell in prudence,
          And I find knowledge and discretion.
          The fear of Yahweh is hatred of evil.
          Pride and arrogance and the way of evil
          And perverted speech I hate.
          I have counsel and sound wisdom;
          I have insight; I have strength.
          By me kings reign and rulers decree what is just;
          By me princes rule, and nobles govern the earth.
          I love those who love me,   *cf. John 3:16*
          And those who seek me diligently find me.   *ref. Isa. 55:6, Matt. 7:7*
          Riches and honor are with me;
          Enduring wealth and prosperity.
          My fruit is better than gold, even fine gold,
          And my yield than choice silver.
          I walk in the way of righteousness, in the paths of justice,
          Endowing with wealth those who love me, and filling their treasuries.

Yahweh <u>created me</u> at the beginning of His work,   *"possessed me"*

the first of His acts of old.   *ref. John 1:1*

Ages ago I was <u>set up</u>,   *"poured out" as an emanation*

at the first, before the beginning of the earth.   *became a reality*

When there were no depths I was brought forth,

When there were no springs abounding with water.

Before the mountains had been shaped,

Before the hills, I was brought forth;

Before He had make the earth with its fields,

Or the first of the dust of the world.

When He established the heavens, I was there;

When He <u>drew a circle</u> on the face of the deep;   *the horizon*

When He made <u>firm</u> the skies above;   *solid <u>firmament</u>*

When He established the <u>fountains of the deep</u>;   *Gen. 7:11*

When He assigned to the sea its limit,

So that the waters might not transgress His command;

When He marked out the <u>foundations of the earth</u>; *Ps. 104:5-7, 2 Sam. 22:8*

Then I was beside Him like a <u>Master Workman</u>; *or little child, one raised up*

And I was daily His delight,   *ref. Col. 1:17, Heb. 1:3*

<u>Rejoicing</u> before Him always;   *Heb. shahaq: playing, fondling:*

Rejoicing in His inhabited world. *living bond between Yahweh and Sophia*

And delighting in the sons of men. *Gen. 26:8, Exod. 32:6, Judges 16:25*

And now, my sons, listen to me:

Happy are those who keep my ways.

Hear instruction and be wise, and do not neglect it.

Happy is the man who listens to me,

Watching daily at my gates,

Waiting beside my doors.

For he who finds me finds life

And obtains favor from Yahweh;

But he who misses me injures himself;

All who hate me love death."

9:1-12   Wisdom has built her house;

She has set up her <u>seven pillars</u>.   *Asherim? house posts? pillars of heaven?*

She has slaughtered her beasts;

She has mixed her wine;

She has also set her table.

She has sent out her maids to call
from the highest places in the town,
"Whoever is simple, let him turn in here!"
To him who is without sense she says,
"Come, eat of my <u>bread</u>   *cf. Eucharist*
And drink of the <u>wine</u> I have mixed.
Leave simpleness, and live,
And walk in the way of insight."
He who corrects a scoffer gets himself abuse,
And he who reproves a wicked man incurs injury.
Do not reprove a scoffer, or he will hate you;
Reprove a wise man, and he will love you.
Give instruction to a wise man, and he will be still wiser;
Teach a righteous man and he will increase in learning.
The fear of Yahweh is the beginning of wisdom,
And the knowledge of <u>the holy</u> (<u>the Holy One</u>) is insight.   *Heb.* Qadosh
For by me your days will be multiplied,   *ref. 30:3 (p. 87)*
And years will be added to your life.
If you are wise, you are wise for yourself;
If you scoff, you alone will bear it.

10:8-10   The wise of heart will heed commandments,
          But a prating fool will come to ruin.
          He who walks in integrity walks securely,
          But he who perverts his ways will be found out.
          He who winks the eye causes trouble,
          But he who boldly reproves makes peace.

10:13   On the lips of him who has understanding wisdom is found,
          But a rod is for the back of him who lacks sense.   *flogging accepted*

10:14   Wise men lay up knowledge,
          But the babbling of a fool brings ruin near.

11:2   When pride comes, then comes disgrace;
          But with the humble is wisdom.

12:1   Whoever loves discipline loves knowledge,
          But he who hates reproof is stupid.

| 12:8 | A man is commended according to his good sense, |
| | But one of perverse mind is despised. |

| 12:15 | The way of a fool is right in his own eyes, |
| | But a wise man listens to advice. |

| 13:1 | A wise son hears his father's instruction, |
| | But a <u>scoffer</u> does not listen to rebuke. | *Heb.* letz.: *scoffer (p. 96)* |

13:14-16	The teaching of the wise is a <u>Fountain of Life</u>,	*ref. 14:27 (p. 1)*
	That one may avoid the snares of death.
	Good sense wins favor,
	But the way of the faithless is their ruin.
	In everything a prudent man acts with knowledge,
	But a fool flaunts his folly.

| 13:18 | The simple acquire folly, | *ref. 14:18 below* |
| | But the prudent are <u>crowned</u> with knowledge. | *14:24 (p. 53)* |

| 13:20 | He who walks with wise men becomes wise, |
| | But the companion of fools will suffer harm. |

14:6-8	A scoffer seeks wisdom in vain,
	But knowledge is easy for a man of understanding.
	Leave the presence of a fool,
	For there you do not meet words of knowledge.
	The wisdom of a prudent man is to discern his way,
	But the folly of fools is deceiving.

| 14:18 | The simple acquire folly, | *"crowned"* |
| | But the prudent are <u>crowned</u> with knowledge. | *Rev. 5:12, 19:12* |

| 14:33 | Wisdom abides in the <u>mind</u> of a man of understanding, | *KJV "heart": leb* |
| | But it is not known in the <u>heart</u> of fools. | *KJV "midst": qereb (center)* |

| 15:2 | The tongue of the wise dispenses knowledge, |
| | But the <u>mouths</u> of fools pour out folly. | *poison tongue, Jas. 3:5,10* |

| 15:7 | The lips of the wise spread knowledge; |
| | Not so the minds of fools. |

15:14   The <u>mind</u> of him who has understanding seeks knowledge,   *KJV "heart"*
         But the <u>mouths</u> of fools feed on folly.

15:21   Folly is a joy to him who has <u>no sense</u>,   *"without heart"*
         But a man of understanding walks aright.   *ref. 6:32 (p. 14)*

16:16   To get wisdom is better than gold;   *ref. 25:11 (p. 86)*
         To get understanding is to be chosen rather than silver.

16:21-24 The wise of <u>heart</u> is called a man of discernment,
         And pleasant speech increases persuasiveness.
         Wisdom is a <u>Fountain of Life</u> to him who has it,   *ref. 14:27 (p. 1)*
         But folly is the chastisement of fools.
         The <u>mind</u> of the wise makes his speech judicious,   *"heart"*
         And adds persuasiveness to his lips,   *eloquent tongue or lips*
         Pleasant words ae like a honeycomb,
         Sweetness to the <u>soul</u> and health to the <u>body</u>.   *breath* (nephesh); *bones*

17:10   A rebuke goes deeper into a man of understanding
         Than a hundred blows into a fool.   *flogging*

17:12   Let a man meet a she-bear robbed of her cubs,
         Rather than a fool in his folly.

17:16   Why should a fool have a price in his hand to buy wisdom,
         When he has no <u>mind</u>?   *KJV "heart to it"*

17:24   A man of understanding sets his face toward wisdom,   *specific goal*
         But the eyes of a fool are on the ends of the earth.   *no target*

17:27-28 He who restrains his words has knowledge,
         And he who has a cool spirit is a man of understanding.
         Even a fool who keeps silent is considered wise;
         When he closes his lips he is deemed intelligent.

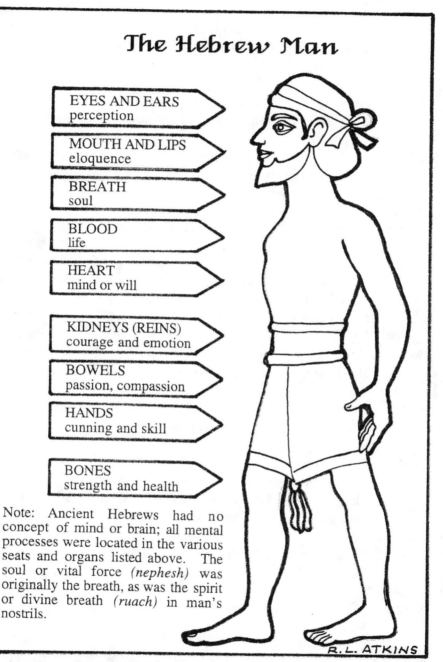

The Hebrew Man

EYES AND EARS
perception

MOUTH AND LIPS
eloquence

BREATH
soul

BLOOD
life

HEART
mind or will

KIDNEYS (REINS)
courage and emotion

BOWELS
passion, compassion

HANDS
cunning and skill

BONES
strength and health

Note: Ancient Hebrews had no concept of mind or brain; all mental processes were located in the various seats and organs listed above. The soul or vital force *(nephesh)* was originally the breath, as was the spirit or divine breath *(ruach)* in man's nostrils.

R.L. ATKINS

The wise of heart is called a man of discernment ... persuasiveness to his lips ... sweetness to the soul (*nephesh*) and health to the body (bones).
(Prov. 16:21-24 [selectively], 10:32 [lips, mouth])

18:1-2 He who is estranged seeks pretexts   *Worthless Opinions:*
     To break out against all sound judgment.   *"sharing" in teenage classes,*
     A fool takes no pleasure in understanding, *shallow "rap sessions" instead of*
     But only in expressing his <u>opinion</u>.   *sound doctrinal instruction*

18:4   The words of a man's mouth are deep waters;
     The fountain of wisdom is a gushing stream. *stream of proverbs (p. xiv)*

18:13   If one gives answer before he hears,   *brash interruption*
     It is his folly and shame.

18:15   An intelligent <u>mind</u> acquires knowledge,   *heart/mind*
     And the ear of the wise seeks knowledge.

19:2-3 It is not good for a man to be without knowledge,
     And he who makes <u>haste</u> with his feet misses his way. *"Haste makes waste."*
     When a man's folly brings his way to ruin,
     His heart rages against Yahweh.

19:8   He who gets wisdom loves himself;   *self-respect vs. low self esteem:*
     He who keeps understanding will prosper. *"Love others as yourself."*

19:10   It is <u>not fitting</u> for a fool to live in luxury, *ref. 26:1 (p. 86), 17:7 (p. 29)*
     Much less for a slave to rule over princes.   *social classes, slaves accepted.*

19:20-21 Listen to advice and accept instruction,
     That you may gain wisdom for the future. *ref. 16:1 (p. 27) determinism:*
     Many are the <u>plans</u> in the mind of a man,   *"Man proposes;*
     But it is the <u>purpose</u> of Yahweh that will be established. *God disposes."*

20:5   The purpose in a man's mind is like deep water, *ulterior motives*
     But a man of understanding will draw it out.

20:12   The hearing ear and the seeing eye,   *understanding and perception*
     Yahweh has made them both.

20:15   There is gold, and abundance of costly stones,
     But the lips of knowledge are a precious jewel. *eloquence in the lips*

20:27   The <u>spirit</u> of man is the lamp of Yahweh,   *conscience is divine introspection*
        Searching all his innermost parts.   *"Know thyself."*
                                        unexamined religion is superstition

21:20   Precious treasure remains in a wise man's dwelling,
        But a foolish man devours it.   *impecunious poverty*

21:22   A wise man scales the city of the mighty   *false confidence*
        And brings down the stronghold in which they trust.   *in weak defenses*

21:30   No wisdom, no understanding, no counsel,   *finite mind vs.*
        Can avail against Yahweh.   *Infinite Mind*

22:17-21   Incline your ear, and hear the <u>words of the Wise</u>,   *"Thirty Sayings of the Wise"*
        And apply your mind to my knowledge;   *based on the Egyptian*
        For it will be pleasant if you keep them within you,   *Instruction of*
        If all of them are ready on your lips.   *Amenemopet*
        That your trust may be in Yahweh,   *with thirty sections.*
        I have made them known to you today, even to you.
        Have I not written for you thirty sayings   *ref.* "Proverbs from
          of admonition and knowledge,   Egypt" *(p. 102)*
          to show you what is right and true,
          that you may give a true answer to those who sent you?

23:9   Do not speak in the hearing of a fool,   *"Do not cast pearls before swine."*
        For he will despise the wisdom of your words.   *Matt. 7:6*

23:12   Apply your <u>mind</u> to instruction
        And your <u>ear</u> to words of knowledge.

23:15-16   My son, if your <u>heart</u> is wise,
        My <u>heart</u> too will be glad.
        My <u>soul</u> will rejoice
        When your lips speak what is right.

23:19   Hear, my son, and be wise,
        And direct your <u>mind</u> in <u>the way</u>.   *cf. Tao (the Way), ref. Acts 19:9*

24:3-7   By wisdom a house is built,
          And by understanding it is established;
          By knowledge the rooms are filled
          With all precious and pleasant riches.
          A wise man is mightier than a strong man,   *The pen is mightier than the sword.*
          And a man of knowledge than he who has strength;
          For by wise guidance you can wage your <u>war</u>,   *war is natural*
          And in abundance of counselors there is <u>victory</u>.
          Wisdom is too high for a fool;
          In the gate he does not open his mouth.

24:9   The <u>devising of folly</u> is sin,
          And the scoffer is an abomination to men.

24:13-14 My son, <u>eat honey</u>, for it is good,   *Rev. 10:10*
          And the drippings of the honeycomb
              are sweet to your taste.   *primitive dietary taboos have*
          Know that wisdom is such to your soul;   *nothing to do with nutrition.*
          If you find it, there will be a future,   *locusts can be eaten, but not*
          And your hope will not be cut off.   *pork, lobsters, rabbits, etc.*

25:11-12 A word fitly spoken   *ref. 16:16 (p. 82), 15:23 (p. 32)*
          Is like apples of gold in a setting of silver.   *Near Eastern esteem for*
          Like a gold ring or an ornament of gold   *aphorisms, proverbs, riddles*
          Is a wise reprover to a listening ear.

25:14   Like clouds and wind without rain
          Is a man who boasts of a gift he does not give.

26:1   Like snow in summer or rain in harvest,
          So honor is not fitting for a fool,   *ref. 19:10 (p. 84)*

26:4-11   <u>Answer not a fool</u> according to his folly,   *An enigma:*
              lest you be like him yourself.   *silence is golden*
          <u>Answer a fool</u> according to his folly,   *silence is yellow.*
              lest he be wise in his own eyes.   *ref. 23:9 (p. 85)*
          He who sends a message by the hand of a fool
              cuts off his own feet and drinks violence.

Like a lame man's legs, which hang useless,
    is a proverb in the mouth of fools.
Like one who binds the stone in the sling
    is he who gives honor to a fool.
Like a thorn that goes up into the hand of a drunkard
    is a proverb in the mouth of fools.
Like an archer who wounds everybody
    is he who hires a passing fool or drunkard.
Like a dog that returns to his vomit   *Insanity: Doing same thing again*
    is a fool that repeats his folly.   *and expecting different results.*

27:12   A prudent man sees danger and hides himself.   *ref. 22:3 (p. 39)*
    But the <u>simple</u> go on and suffer for it.   *"simple": Heb. pethi (p. 96)*

27:22   Crush a <u>fool</u> in a mortar with a pestle along with crushed grain;
    Yet his folly will not depart from him.   *"fool": Heb. kesil (p. 96)*

28:26   He who trusts in his own mind is a fool,   *anti-intellectualism*
    But he who walks in wisdom will be delivered.

29:8-9   <u>Scoffers</u> set a city aflame,   *"scoffer": Heb. letz (p. 96)*
    But wise men turn away wrath.
If a wise man has an argument with a <u>fool</u>,
The fool only rages and laughs, and there is no quiet.

29:11   A <u>fool</u> gives full vent to his anger,   *self control is maturity*
    But a wise man quietly holds it back.

29:20   Do you see a man who is hasty in his words?   *medieval choleric humor*
    There is more hope for a <u>fool</u> than for him.

30:2-3   Surely I am too stupid to be a man.   *words of Agur, not Solomon (p. xvi)*
    I have not the understanding of a man.
I have not learned wisdom,   *"holiness": Heb. qadoshim*
Nor have I knowledge of <u>holiness</u>.   *"The Holy One": Qadosh Echod*
    (p. 98)

30:24-28   Four things on earth are small,
           But they are exceedingly wise: *Wisdom allows adaptation*
           The <u>ants</u> are a people not strong,
               yet they provide their food in the summer;   *cf. Aesop's fables*
           The <u>badgers</u> are a people not mighty,
               yet they make their homes in the rocks;
           The <u>locusts</u> have no king,
               yet all of them march in rank;
           The <u>lizard</u> you can take in your hands,
               yet it is in king's palaces.

WOMEN

11:22   Like a gold ring in a swine's snout
            Is a beautiful woman without discretion.

14:1   Wisdom builds her house,   *ref. 14:1 (p. 17)*
            But Folly with her own hands tears it down.
                  (The whore in Scripture: Ezek. 16:28-29, 35-37; Hos. 1:2; Rev. 17:3-5)

18:22   He who finds a wife finds a good thing   *ref. 31:10-31 (p. 7), the good wife*
            And obtains favor <u>from Yahweh</u>.

19:13b   ... and a wife's quarreling is a continual dripping of rain.   *ref. 19:13 (p. 3)*

19:14   House and wealth are inherited from fathers,
            But a prudent wife is <u>from Yahweh</u>.   *a marriage made in heaven*

21:9   It is better to live in a corner of the housetop
            Than in a house shared with a contentious woman.

21:19   It is better to live in a desert land
            Than with a contentious and fretful woman.

25:24   It is better to live in a corner of the housetop
            Than in a house shared with a contentious woman.

27:15-16 A continual dripping on a rainy day
            And a contentious woman are alike.
            To restrain her is to restrain the wind   *Hos. 8:7, John 3:8*
            Or to grasp oil in his right hand.

30:18-19 Three things are too wonderful for me;
            Four I do not understand: *Mysteries of life:*
            The way of an eagle in the sky,   *how to fly like a bird*
            The way of a serpent on a rock,   *having wisdom and cunning*
            The way of a ship on the high seas, and   *how to safely go over water*
            The way of a man with a maiden.   *understanding love and sex*

31:1b-3   ... which his mother taught him: *words of Lemuel (31:1) (p. xvi)*
           What, my son?
           What, son of my womb?
           What, son of my vows?   *sexual euphemisms:*
           Give not your <u>strength</u> to women,   *semen (sexual lassitude)*
           Your <u>ways</u> to those who destroy kings.   *thigh (sexual member)*

                              "strength": ref. 5:10 (p. 13), "Ways": ref. 5:8 (p. 13)

... the way of a man with a maiden.
(Prov. 30:19)

APPENDIX

ALPHABETIC ACROSTICS IN THE BIBLE

The use of acrostics and hidden cyphers in the Bible is widespread, an indication of the type of clever composition and inventiveness that some writers used to manipulate the divine message. Acrostics and other poetic word groupings were utilized for a number of reasons such as literary effect (ostentation), mnemonic purposes (to aid in memorizing the passage), and out of a primitive reverence for the letters of the alphabet.

Among the ancients there was a feeling that because knowledge was written using letters of the alphabet, a simple listing of items in that alphabet "from A to Z" was a way of summerizing all human knowledge. It is for this reason that the New Testament speaks of Christ as "the Alpha and Omega, the Beginning and the End."

It was also thought that literate persons could possess occult powers: A wizard who could "spell" was able to cast a *spell*.; a seer who could "read" was able to *rede* the future. Magic charms were made by scrambling letters into incantations such as "Abracadabra," which was devised from the name of the Gnostic rooster god *Abraxas*. Similarly, the magician's "hocus pocus" came from the Latin invocation of the Catholic mass *Hoc Est Corpus Meum*, "This is My Body," which changes bread into flesh.

Prior to the invention of Arabic numerals, the mystery of letters was enhanced by the fact that they doubled as numbers. This property of letters introduced the practice of calculating the value of a word by adding up the numerical values of its letters. For example, the name "Nero Caesar" has the numerical equivalent of "666." This "science" of numerology is also called gematria (a corruption of "geometry").

Acrostics, such as those below, have a charm that has lasted through the ages:

MOTHER
Many things she gave me;
Only that she's growing **O**ld;
Tears she shed to save me;
Heart of purest gold;
Eyes with love-light shining;
Right and right she'll always be.
Put them all together; they spell MOTHER,
A word that means the world to me.

FAITH is: **F**orsaking **A**ll **I** **T**ake **H**im.

GRACE is: **G**od's **R**iches **A**t **H**is Expense.

One of the most well-known acrostics is that of Psalm 119, because in some versions of the Bible Hebrew letters are inserted between each of the eight-line stanzas—all the lines which begin with that letter. To show how this was done in the original, the following arrangement of the first two stanzas is paraphrased to make each line begin with the first two letters of the Roman alphabet.

Psalm 119
("The Perfect Law" from *Aleph* to *Tav*)

A (Aleph)

Always happy are those whose way is blameless,
  who walk in the law of Yahweh.
Always happy are those who keep His testimonies,
  who seek Him with their whole heart,
Also doing no wrong, but walking in His ways.
And You have commanded Your precepts to be kept diligently.
Ah, that my ways may be steadfast in keeping Your statutes.
As a result, I shall not be put to shame,
  having my eyes fixed on all Your commandments.
An upright heart in me will praise You,
  when I learn Your righteous ordinances.
As I observe Your statutes, do not forsake me utterly.

B (Beth)

But how can a young man keep his way pure?
  By guarding it according to Your word.
Because I seek You with all my heart,
  Let me not wander from Your commandments.
Because I have laid up Your word in my heart,
  I must not sin against You.
Blessed are You, O Yahweh; teach me Your statutes.
By my lips are spoken all the ordinances of Your mouth.
Being in the way of Your testimonies,
  I find delight as much as in all riches.
By meditation on Your precepts I will fix my eyes on Your ways.
Bountiful joy is mine in Your statutes;
  I will not forget Your word.

Similar literary styles occur elsewhere in the Bible:

Lamentations, chapters 1–4: Every verse begins with a successive letter in the 22-letter Hebrew alphabet. In chapter 3, each letter is repeated three times. (This peculiar, poetic form of expressing grief seems rather artificial.)

Psalms 9, 10: Every other verse has a successive letter. (Psalms 9 and 10 are one Psalm in the Septuagint.)

Psalms 25, 34, 111, 112, 145: Every verse has a successive letter.

Psalm 37: Every other verse has a successive letter.

Proverbs 31:10-30: The virtues of a perfect wife, from A to V, is given. A paraphrase of this passage is given below, in which the Roman letters from A to V stand for the 22 letters of the Hebrew alphabet.

The Perfect Wife

A good wife, who can find?
　She is more precious than jewels.
Boundless trust is in her husband's heart,
　And he will have no lack of good things.
Caring for him all the days of her life,
　She does him good and never harm.
Diligently she seeks wool and flax
　And works with willing hands.
Earnestly searching like the ship of a merchant,
　She brings her food from afar.
Food is provided for her husband and tasks for her maids,
　When she rises before dawn.
Going out to inspect a field, she buys it,
　And with her own hands she plants a vineyard.
Her arms are girded with strength,
　And her hands are ever busy.
Industry ensures that her merchandise is profitable,
　And her lamp stays burning at night.
Just as tirelessly she twirls the distaff,
　And her hand works the spindle.

Kindly she opens her hand to the poor,
   And reaches out to help the needy.
Lightly she regards the snow and cold, for her family
   Is all clothed in scarlet.
Making all of her own clothing,
   Her garments are all fine linen and purple.
Numbered among the officials at the gates,
   Her husband sits among the elders of the land.
Out of the excess material she makes linen garments for sale;
   She delivers embroidery to the shop keepers.
Pride and dignity are her clothing,
   And she laughs at the time to come.
Questions about her wisdom never arise,
   And the teaching of kindness is on her tongue.
Regarding always the benefit of her household,
   She does not eat the bread of idleness.
She is blessed by her children,
   And her husband also praised her:
There are many fine women in the world,
   But you surpass them all!
Ultimately, charm is deceitful, and beauty is vain,
   But a woman who has reverence for God is to be praised.
Value her; give her the rewards of her diligence,
   And let her works praise her in the gates.

This is the ideal Hebrew housewife "from *Aleph* to *Tav.*"

HEBREW CONCEPTS

Hebrew Terms for Foolish Persons:

Kesil (or *Ewil*): Thickness, Fatness (like a pig), Lowbrow, Loudmouth.
Pethi: Naive, Pliable, Untutored Youth, Greenhorn.
Letz: Scoffer, Scorner, Mocker, Sacrilegious, Insolent, Know-it-all, Opinionated, Disrepectful of sacred values.
Chaser Lev: Having No Heart (no sense).
Atsel: Slothful, Indolent

The Tree of Life—a Date Palm:

He [Yahweh] drove out the man. And at the east of the Garden of Eden he placed the Cherubs, and a flaming Sword which turned every way, to guard the way to the Tree of Life.
(Gen. 3:24)

He [Solomon] carved all the walls of the house [temple] round about with carved figures of Cherubs and Palm Trees and open flowers in the inner and outer rooms.
(1 Kgs. 6:29)

... And on all the walls round about in the inner room and the nave were carved likenesses of Cherubs and Palm Trees, a Palm Tree between Cherub and Cherub...
(Ezek. 41:17b-18a)

So they took branches of Palm Trees and went out to meet Him, crying "Hosanna, Blessed is He who comes in the name of the Lord, even the King of Israel!"
(John 12:13)

The Fountain of Life—a Paradise Oasis:

A River flowed out of Eden to water the garden, and there is divided and became four Rivers.
(Gen. 2:10)

Then he brought me back to the door of the Temple, and, behold, water was issuing from below the threshold of the Temple toward the east...
(Ezek.) 47:1a

Then he showed me the River of the Water of Life, bright as crystal, flowing from the throne of God and of the Lamb through the middle of the street of the city. Also, on either side of the River, the Tree of Life ...
(Rev. 22:1-2a)

"The Temple"   R. ATKINS

HOLY NAMES OF GOD

"No man knows how to know Him. His Name remains hidden. His Name is a mystery to His children. His Names are innumerable. They are manifold, and none know their number."

(*Egyptian Religion*, Wallis Budge)

EH-YEH (I Am)

YAHWEH (yah-weh), יהוה (*YHWH*, Tetragrammaton) Self-Existent One, He Who Exists, He Who Causes to Exist, Jehovah, Yah (Exod. 6:3)

YAHWEH SABAOTH: Yahweh of Hosts, Armies, Angel Warriors

HA SHEM (The Name)

ELOHIM (el-o-heem): God, Godhead, plural, gods (Gen. 1:1)

EL (*Theos*, God)

ELOHI-ZEBAOT (*Yahweh Sabaoth*, Lord of Hosts)

EL SHADDAI (ale shad-dah-ee): God of Mountains, KJV God Almighty (Gen. 17:1, 28:3; Exod. 6:3; Num. 24:16). Equivalent to Greek *Pantokrator*.

EL ELYON (ale el-yone): God Most High (Gen. 14:18, Num. 24:16, Ps. 91:1, Isa. 14:14, Dan. 3:26)

EL OLAM (ale o-lahm): God Everlasting, God of the Universe (Gen. 21:33, Isa. 40:28)

EL QADOSH (ale kah-doshe): Holy God (Isa. 5:16)

EL ROIY (ale ro-ee): God of Seeing (Gen. 16:13)

EL BERITH (ale b'rith): God of the Covenant (Judges 9:46)

EL EMUNAH (ale eh-mu-nah): God of Faithfulness (Deut. 32:4)

EL PACHAD (ale pakh-ahd): God of Fear (Job 31:23, Gen. 31:42, 53)

EL BETHEL (ale beth-ale): God of the House of God (Gen. 35:7)

ADONAI (ah-do-nah-ee): Lord (Gen. 15:2). Equivalent to Canaanite *Ba'al*, Babylonian *Bel*, Greek *Kyrios*, Latin *Dominus*   Holy, Holy, Holy

TSADDIYQ ECHAD (tsahd-deek ekh-ahd): Righteous One (Isa. 24:16)

QADOSH ECHAD (kah-doshe ekh-ahd): Holy Unity (2 Kgs. 19:22; Ps. 71:22, 89:7, 18; Prov. 30:3; Isa. 1:4, 5:16, 19, 10:17, 12:6, 17:7; Hos. 11:9, 12)

MELEK (meh-lek): King (Jer. 10:7, 10; Zeph. 3:15; Zech. 14:17; Mal. 1:14) Equivalent to Canaanite *Melk*, *Milcom*, *Moloch*

MELECH HA OLAM (King of the Universe)

EBEN (ev-en): Rock (Gen. 49:24, Isa. 17:10, 2 Sam. 23:3)

EBENEZER (ev-en-ee-zer): Rock of Help (1 Sam. 4:1, 5:1, 7:12)

AB (ahv): Father (Ps. 89:26, Isa. 9:6) Equivalent to Aramaic *Abba*.

Abrahum

↳ Abram to Abraham

ASAH (ah-sah): Maker (Ps. 95:6, 149:2; Prov. 14:31, 17:5; Isa. 17:7; Hos. 8:14)

BARA, BOREY (bo-ray): Creator (Eccl. 12:1; Isa. 40:28, 43:15)

ATTIYQ (aht-teek): Ancient One, Ancient of Days (Dan. 7:9,13)

SHIYLOH (shee-lo): Tranquil, Secure (Gen. 49:10)

ABIYR (ah-beer): Mighty One (Gen. 49:24, Ps. 99:4)

RA'AH (rah-ah): Shepherd (Gen. 49:24, Ps. 23:1)

SHAPHAT (shah-faht): Judge (Gen. 18:25, Judges 11:27)

QANNA (kahn-nah): Jealous (Exod. 34:14)

AZ (ahz): Majesty, Power (Ps. 59:9,17; Isa. 12:2) — WIZARD OF OZ

NETSACH (nay-tsahk): Strength (1 Sam. 15:29)

YASHA (yah-shah): Savior, Deliverer (Ps. 106:21, Isa. 43:3)   "IKHABOD"

GA'AL (gah-ahl): Redeemer (Job 19:25, Prov. 23:1)

KABOD (kah-vode): Glory, Splendor, Weight (1 Sam. 2:8, 4:21, 6:5; Ezek. 8:4, 9:3)

PANIYM (pah-neem): Presence, Face, Countenance (Ps. 68:8)

YARAH (yaw-raw): Teacher (Isa. 30:20)

YAH YIREH (yah-yireh): Yah will provide, Yah will see (to it), alt. name of Mt. Moriah.

JEWISH KABBALA SEPHIROTH

AYN SOF (Endless One, *Zervan Ankara*: Eternal Time)

KETHER (Crown), *ATTIYQ* (Ancient of Days), White Head, The Primordial Point,
   Ahura Mazda (Wise Lord)

ARIKH APHIM (*Macroprosopus*, Great Countenance)

HOKMAH (*Sophia*, Wisdom), *ABBA* (Father), *DAVAR* (*Memra, Logos*, Word),

BINAH (Understanding, Reason), *AYMA* (Mother),

SHEKINAH (Presence), *HA YAM* (The Sea), *Matronit*, Queen

ZAUIR ANPIN (*Microprosopus*, Lesser Countenance), *DAATH* (Knowledge)

HESED (Mercy, Steadfast Love), *GEDULAH* (Greatness, Kindness, Love)

GEVURAH (Power, Strength, Severity), *PACHAD* (Terror)

TIPHERETH (Beauty, Glory)

NETZACH (Firmness, Might, Victory, Eternity)

HOD (Splendor, Majesty), *KAVOD* (Glory)

YESOD (Root, Foundation, Principle, *Organum Sanctitatis*)

MALCUTH (Kingdom, Sovereignty), ZION, The Bride, The Queen, Mother Nature,
   Anima Mundi

YALDABAOTH (*Yah-El-Adonai-Sabaoth*, Gnostic Demiurge)

Yahweh, Redeemer, Holy One (Isa. 43:14)

Yahweh, Holy One, Creator, King (Isa. 43:15)

I Am He (Isa. 43:25, 46:4, 48:12, 51:12)

I Am First and Last (Isa. 48:12)

I Am God (Isa. 46:9)

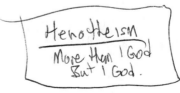

Henotheism
More than 1 God
But 1 God.

Arch Angels FM ZOROASTRIANS
Khalil — FRIEND

POETIC PARALLELISM
IN THE HEBREW SCRIPTURES

The second line repeats the first line in slightly altered phraseology. This construction is a mark of Hebrew poetry.

Judah, your brothers shall praise you...
Your father's sons shall bow down before you.
(Gen. 49:8)

The scepter shall not depart from Judah,
Nor the ruler's staff from between his feet.
(Gen. 49:10)

Thy rod (comforts me), and
Thy staff comforts me.   *two terms for just one shepherd's crook*
(Ps. 23:4)

He Who sits in the heavens laughs;
Yahweh has them in derision.
(Ps. 2:4)

Show me Your ways, O Yahweh;
Teach me Your paths.
(Ps. 25:4)

What is man that You should think of him
And the son of man that You should care for him?
(Ps. 8:4)

Hear, my son, your father's instruction,
And do not reject your mother's teaching.
(Prov. 1:8)

Behold, your King comes:
Riding on an ass, *cf. Matt. 21:2 vs. Mark 11:2,*
And on a colt, the foal of an ass. *Luke 19:30, John 12:14)*
(Zech. 9:9)

Their tongue is sharp as a snake's tongue; *paraphrase*
Under their lips is a snake's poison.
(Ps. 140:3)

You snakes (serpents),
You offspring of snakes (brood of vipers)...
(Matt. 23:33)

PROVERBS FROM EGYPT

One section of the Book of Proverbs (22:17–24:22) is closely related to an ancien
Egyptian manuscript called *The Instruction of Amenemopet*. The Egyptian proverbialis
identifies himself as a scribe and "the Overseer of Grains, who regulates the measur
and manages the yield of grain for his lord, who registers islands and newly appearing
lands in the great name of his majesty." Parallels are given below:

Amenemopet

Give your <u>ears</u> and <u>hear</u> what is said,
Give your <u>heart</u> to understand them.
To put them <u>in your heart</u> is
  worth while.
(3:8-11)

Books of Proverbs

Incline your <u>ear</u> and <u>hear</u> the Words
  of the Wise,
And apply your <u>heart</u> to my knowledge;
For it will be pleasant if you keep them
  <u>within you</u> ...
(22:17-18a)

Leave him (the wicked) in the arms
  of the god;
Fill his belly with your <u>bread</u>, so that
  he may be sated and may be ashamed.
(5:4-6)

If your enemy is hungry, give him <u>bread</u>
  to eat, and if he is thirsty, give him
  water to drink;
For you will heap coals of fire on his head,
And Yahweh will reward you.
(25:21-22)

Do not carry off the <u>landmark</u> at the
  boundaries of the arable land,
Nor disturb the position of the
  measuring cord;
Be not greedy for a cubit of land,
Nor encroach upon the boundaries
  of a <u>widow</u> ...
(7:12-15)

Do not remove an ancient <u>landmark</u>
Or enter the fields of the <u>fatherless</u>;
(23:10)

Lest a terror carry you off,...
  one who determines the boundaries
  of the arable land.
(8:10-12)

For their redeemer is strong;
He will plead their cause against you.
(23:11)

Better is bread when the heart
  is happy,
Than riches with sorrow.
(9:7-8)

Better is a little with the fear of Yahweh
Than great treasure and trouble with it.
Better is a dinner of herbs where love is
Than a fatted ox and hatred with it.
(15:16-17)

If riches are brought to you by robbery,
They will not spend the night with you.
At daybreak they are not in your house;
... they have made themselves wings
  like geese
And have flown away to the heavens.
(9:16-18, 10:4-5)

Do not toil to acquire wealth;
Be wise enough to desist.
When your eyes light upon it,
  it is gone;
For suddenly it takes to itself wings,
Flying like an eagle toward heaven.
(23:4-5)

Do not associate yourself to the heated
  man, nor visit him for conversation.
(22:24)

Make no friendship with a man of anger,
Nor go with a wrathful man
(10:16-17)

Do not lean on the scales
  nor falsify the weights,
  nor damage the fractions of measure.
(16:15-16)

Diverse weights are an abomination
  to Yahweh,
And false scales are not good.
(20:23)

The ape god sits beside the balance
And his heart is in the plummet.
Which god is as great as Thoth,
He that discovered these things,
  to make them?
Make not for yourself weights that
  are deficient.
They bring great grief through the
  will of the god.
(17:22f)

A just balance and scales are Yahweh's;
All the weights in the bag are His work.
(16:11)

The words that men say are one thing;
That which the god does is another.
(19:16-17)

The plans of the mind belong to man,
But the answer of the tongue is from
  Yahweh.
(16:1)

Many are the plans in the mind of man,
But it is the purpose of Yahweh
  that will be established.
(19:21)

Note: Thomas a Kempis said: "Man proposes, but God disposes."
(Latin: *Homo proposuit sed Deus disponit.*)

Do not accept the bribe of a
  powerful man,
Nor oppress the disabled for him.
(21:3-4)

A wicked man accepts a bribe from
  the bosom
To pervert the ways of justice.
(17:23)

Do not say, "I have found a patron,
  for one who hates me has injured me."
For surely you do not know the plans
  of the god.
Lest you be ashamed tomorrow,
Sit yourself down in the hands of the god
And your silence will cast them down.
(22:3-8)

Do not say, "I will repay evil."
Wait for Yahweh, and He will help you.
(20:22)

Do not boast about tomorrow,
For you do not know what a day
  may bring forth.
(27:1)

Do not spread your words to
  the common people,
Do not associate to yourself one
  (who is too) outgoing of heart.
(22:13-14)

Do not speak in the hearing of a fool,
For he will despise the wisdom of your
  words.
(23:9)

He who goes about gossiping
  reveals secrets;
Therefore, do not associate with one
  who speaks foolishly.
(20:19)

Better is a man whose talk (stays)
  in his belly,
Than he who proclaims it injuriously.
(22:15-16)

A prudent man conceals his knowledge,
But fools proclaim their folly.
(12:23)

Do not eat bread before a nobleman,
Nor lay on your mouth at first...
Observe the cup that is before you,
And let it serve your needs.
(23:13-18)

When you sit down to eat with a ruler,
Observe carefully what is before you,
And put a knife to your throat,
If you are a man given to appetite.
Do not desire his delicacies,
For they are deceptive food.
(23:1-3)

Do you see these thirty chapters;
They entertain and they instruct.
They are the foremost of all books;
They make the ignorant to know.
(27:7-10)

Have I not written for you thirty sayings
   of admonition and knowledge,
To show you what is right and true,
That you may give a true answer
   to those who sent you?
(22:20-21)

As for the scribe who is experienced
   in his office,
He will find himself worthy (to be)
   a courtier.
(27:16-17)

Do you see a man skilful in his work?
He will stand before kings;
He will not stand before obscure men.
(22:29)

A verse-by-verse comparison is given by Simpson:

Amenemopet	Proverbs
3:9-11, 3:16 (Chapter 1)	22:17-18
1:7 (Introductory)	22:19
27:7-8 (Chapter 30)	22:20
1:5-6 (Introductory)	22:21
4:4-5 (Chapter 2)	22:22
no parallel	22:23
11:13-14 (Chapter 9)	22:24
13:8-9 (Chapter 9)	22:25
no parallel	22:26-27
7:12-13 (Chapter 6)	22:28
27:16-17 (Chapter 30)	22:29
23:13-18 (Chapter 23)	23:1-3
9:14-10:5 (Chapter 7)	23:4-5
14:5-10 (Chapter 11)	23:6-7
14:17-18 (Chapter 11)	23:8
22:11-12 (Chapter 21)	23:9
7:12-15, 8:9-10 (Chapter 6)	23:10-11
no parallels	23:12-24:10
1:6-7 (Chapter 8)	24:11
no parallels	24:12-22

SOPHIA (ΣΩΦΙΑ): WISDOM

I, Wisdom, dwell in prudence and grasp knowledge and discretion ... Jehovah created Me at the beginning of His work, the first of His acts of old. Ages ago I was set up, at the first, before the beginning of the earth ... When He established the heavens, I was there. When He drew a circle on the face of the cosmic Deep, when He made firm the skies above...Then I was daily His delight, playing before Him always. (Prov. 8:12, 22-23, 27-28a, 30b-31a)   ≈ ZOROASTRIANISM

I came forth from the mouth of the Most High and covered the earth like a mist. I dwelt in high places, and My throne was in a pillar of cloud. Alone I have made the circuit of the vault of heaven and have walked in the depths of the cosmic Deep ... From eternity, in the beginning, He created Me, and for eternity I shall not cease to exist. (Sirach 24:3-5, 9)

For Wisdom is more mobile than any motion ... for She is a Spirit of the Power of God, and a pure Emanation of the Glory of the Almighty...For She is more beautiful than the sun and excels every constellation of the stars. Compared with the light She is found to be superior, for it is succeeded by the night, but against Wisdom evil does not prevail... She glorifies her noble birth by living with God, and the Lord of all loves Her. (Wisdom 7:24a, 25a, 29-30)

God is...the Father of all things ... and the Husband of Wisdom, sowing for the race of mankind the Seed of happiness in good and virgin soil. (Philo Judaeus, *De Cherubim*, xiv: 49)

And a great portent appeared in heaven, a Woman clothed with the sun, with the moon under Her feet, and on Her head a crown of twelve stars. She was with Child... (Rev. 12:1)

Therefore, also, the Wisdom of God said "I will send them profites and apostles, Some of whom they will Kill and persecute." Compare Math 23:34 Luke

TABULATION OF SCRIPTURES

Chapter 13	
1	2, 81
2-3	20
4	66
5	20
6	61
7-8	52
9	35
10	50
11	67
12	32
13	43
14-16	81
17	21
18	52, 81
19	32
20	81
21-22	35
22	52
23	46
24	3
25	53

Chapter 14	
1	17, 89
2	61
3	50
4	53
5	21
6-8	81
9	63
10	46
11-14	36
15	21
16	63
17	9
18	81
19-20	53
21-22	46
23	67
24	53
25	21
26	1
27	1
28	53
29	10
30	36
31	46
32	36

33	81
34	63
35	53

Chapter 15	
1	10
2	81
3	36
4	21
5	37
6	53
7	81
8-12	37
13	32
14	82
15	32
16-17	53
18	10
19	67
20	3
21	82
22	44
23	32
24	37
25	50
26	63
27	53
28	63
29	37
30	32
31-32	37
33	1

Chapter 16	
1	27
2-4	37
5	50
6	46, 63
7	37
8	53
9	27
10	29
11	37
12-15	29
16	82
17	63
18-19	50
20	32
21-24	82

25	38
26	67
27-30	21
31	63
32	10
33	27

Chapter 17	
1	32
2	3
3	38
4	21
5	46
6	38
7	21, 29
8-9	46
9	10
10	82
11	38
12	82
13	38
14	10
15	38
16	82
17	48
18	53
19	10
20	21
21	3
22	32
23	44
24	82
25	3
26	38
27-28	82

Chapter 18	
1-2	84
3	38
4	84
5-7	38
8	21
9	54
10	63
11-12	50
13	84
14	32
15	84
16	48

17-19	38
20-21	21
22	89
23	54
24	48

Chapter 19

1	22
2-3	84
4	54
5	22
6	48
7	54
8	84
9	22
10	84
11	10
12	29
13	3, 89
14	89
15	67
16	43
17	46
18	3
19	39
20-21	84
22	22
23	63
24	67
25	39
26-27	3
28	22
29	39

Chapter 20

1	71
2	29
3	10
4	67
5	84
6	48
7	63
8	29
9	63
10	17
11	63
12	84
13	67
14	54

15	84
16	54
17	22
18	29
19	22
20	3
21	54
22	39
23	17
24	27
25	2
26	29
27	85
28	29
29	3
30	39

Chapter 21

1	27
2	64
3	39
4	50
5	67
6-7	18
8	64
9	89
10	48
11-12	39
13-14	98
15-16	39
17	54
18	39
19	89
20	85
21	64
22	85
23	22
24	50
25-26	67
27	70
28	22
29	64
30	85
31	39

Chapter 22

1-2	54
3	39
4	54

5	40
6	3
7	54
8	40
9	48
10	10
11	30
12	40
13	67
14	17
15	3
16	54
17-21	85
17	2
22-23	18
24-25	10
26-29	55

Chapter 23

1-8	55
9	85
10-11	55
12	85
13-14	5
15-16	85
17-18	64
19	85
20-21	71
22	5
23	22
24-25	64
26	5
27-28	17
29-35	71

Chapter 24

1-2	24
3-7	86
8	10
9	86
10-12	48
13-14	86
15	64
16-18	40
19	24
20	40
21-22	30
23-26	44
23	2

27	55
28	44
29	48
30-34	69

Chapter 25

1	2
2-3	30
4	18
5-8	30
9-10	49
11-12	86
13	22
14	86
15	30
16	56
17	69
18-19	22
20	32
21-22	49
23	10
24	89
25	56
26	64
27	56
28	11

Chapter 26

1	86
2-3	40
-11	86
12	50
13-16	69
17	11
18-25	24
26-27	40
28	24

Chapter 27

1,2	27, 51
3-6	11
7-8	57
9-10	49
11	5
12	87
13	57
14	24
15-16	89
17	49

18	57
19	49
20	24
21	49
22	87
23-27	57

Chapter 28

1	64
2	30
3	57
4	43
5	40
6	64
7	43
8	18
9	43
10	40
11	51
12-14	64
15-16	30
17	11
18	65
19	69
20	57
21	41
22	57
23	24
24	5
25	51
26	87
27	49
28	65

Chapter 29

1	41
2	65
3	17
4	30
5	24
6-7	65
8-9	87
10	65
11	87
12	31
13	49
14	31
15	5
16	65

17	5
18	43
19	41
20	87
21	5
22	11
23	51
24	18
25	41
26	31
27	65

Chapter 30

1	2
2-3	87
4	1
5-6	43
7-9a	1, 24
9b	2
10	57
11	5
12	65
13	51
14	57
15-16	25
17	5
18-19	89
20	17
21-23	51
24-28	88
29-31	31
32	51
33	11

Chapter 31

1-3	90
4-5	71
6-7	72
8-9	41
10-31	7

CPSIA information can be obtained
at www.ICGtesting.com
Printed in the USA
FSHW022133011120

9 781635 281262